EL GRECO

EL GRECO

Doménico Theotocópuli

PHILIP TROUTMAN

MARBORO BOOKS · NEW YORK

ACKNOWLEDGMENTS

The pieces and paintings in this volume are reproduced by kind permission of the following collections and galleries to which they belong: Church of Santo Domingo el Antiguo, Toledo (Plate ix); Church of Santo Tomé, Toledo (Plate xvii); Cincinnati Art Museum (Plate xxxiv); Dumbarton Oaks, Washington, D.C. (Plate xliv); Estense Gallery, Modena (Plates i, ii, iii); Hospital de la Caridad, Illescas (xxxviii, xxxix, xl, xli); Institute of Art, Chicago (Plate vii); Johnson Collection, Philadelphia (Plate vi); Metropolitan Museum of Art, New York (Plates xxix, xxxii, xlviii); Minneapolis Institute of Art (Plate v); Monastery of the Escorial (Plates xii, xiii, xlv); Mrs Maxwell MacDonald, Pollok House, Glasgow (Plate xi); Museo del Greco, Toledo (Plate xxxvii); Museo di Capodimonte, Naples (Plate iv); Museum of Fine Arts, Boston, Mass. (Plate xlii); National Gallery, London (Plate xxxi); National Gallery, Washington D.C. (Plates xxvii, xxviii, xxx, xlvi); Nelson Gallery, Kansas City, (Plate xv); Palencia Cathedral (Plate xiv); Museo del Prado, Madrid (Plates viii, xix, xx, xxii, xxiii, xxiv, xxv, xxxiii); Museo Provincial, Seville (Plate xxxvi); Rumanian National Museum, Bucharest (Plates xxi, xlvii); Museo de Santa Cruz, Toledo (x, xvi, xviii, xxvi, xliii); Toledo Museum of Art, Ohio (Plate xxxiv). The black and white photographs in this volume are reproduced by kind permission of the following collections and galleries to which the belong: The Metropolitan Museum of Art, New York, (Frontispiece); Frick Collection (Fig. 2); Hospital de Taverna (Fig. 3); M.H. de Young Memorial Museum, San Francisco (Fig. 1) Museo del Greco, Toledo (Figs. 4, 5); Museo del Prado, Madrid (Fig. 6); The following photographs were supplied by Michael Holford: (Plates viii, ix, xii, xiii, xvi, xcii, xix, xxii, xxiii, xxiv, xxv, xxvi, xxxi, xxxiii, xxxviii, xxxix, xl, xli, xliii, xlv); by Scala, Florence: (Plates ii, xx); by Ramos, Madrid: (Plate xxxvii).

Published by
MARBORO BOOKS
131 Varick Street • New York, 13, N. Y.
By arrangement with
Paul Hamlyn Ltd., London
© Paul Hamlyn Ltd 1963
Printed in Czechoslowakia
T 1278

Contents

Black and White

Introduction

'*Crete gave him his life . . .*' (Paravicino, on the death of El Greco, 1614.)

The first great Spanish painter was not a native of Spain, but of the Greek island of Crete in the eastern Mediterranean. If the testimony he made towards the end of his life is true, Domenicos Theotocopoulos — for that was his name — was born in 1540 or 1541. Even this, however, is open to some doubt, for all other indications are that he was born some few years later. In vain we seek to know something of the young Domenicos in Crete, where it seems he spent his childhood and his youth, but there is absolutely no information.

One thing is certain, that those years on the Greek island made a deep and permanent impression upon him; an impression concealed during the years of his early manhood spent in Italy in examining the infinity of new impressions of Western Renaissance culture, but whose spirit is remembered in his later years when he was so far from the land of his birth. It is the significance of his Byzantine and medieval origins that Paravicino, the great Toledan poet, acknowledges in his sonnet written on the passing of his friend, the great 'Toledan' painter.

While nothing is known of his parents, or of the Theotocopoulos family, there is every indication that his family was of some status, and able at least to provide a liberal education for Domenicos. It is clear that he was given a thorough schooling in the Greek language and letters, a study which he was to cultivate throughout his life. Francisco Pacheco, the erudite painter and poet from Seville, Velasquez' master and father-in-law, who visited the aged El Greco in Toledo in 1611, tells us he was a 'great philosopher, quick and discerning in his remarks', and the library left on his death contained many works of the Greek philosophers and poets as well as devotional works in his native tongue. There is the same evidence that in Italy he applied himself to the study of the Italian philosophers and poets.

It was almost certainly in Crete, too, that he received his first artistic training, and possibly in the monastery of Saint Catherine, the most important school of painting on the island, to which he seems to make reference in the first work known by his hand, the *Modena Triptych*, painted in Italy. Monasteries were the only places of learning and artistic training in Crete, still medieval in its culture and linked with the East, and little affected by the great Renaissance in Italy. In Italy the past two and a half centuries had seen the establishment of an entirely new culture, and all the Western world was awake to the new ideas, but in Crete, Byzantine art still flourished — the kind of art practised in Italy by Duccio, who had died some two hundred years before.

The grand, hieratic, abstract images of Byzantine art, in mosaic or miniature, powerful and impressive in their design and colour, had the authority of a millennium of development, and were the expression of the spirit of a whole society. A comparable impression and authority speak from the designs of El Greco's maturity. We shall probably never know what his Cretan paintings were like. If indeed he was trained as a painter in Crete, they would have been very different from his earliest known works, painted soon after his arrival in Italy.

'A young pupil of Titian's . . .' (Giulio Clovio, letter to Cardinal Farnese, 1570.)
At the end of the fifteenth century, in the reign of the Catholic sovereigns, Ferdinand and Isabella, the Moors were finally expelled from their last dominion in Spain, some seven hundred years after their first invasion of the peninsula; at the same time there began the real invasion, in the eastern Mediterranean, of Europe by the Turks, that was not to be halted until it reached Vienna. The incursion of the Turks, which threatened Crete, encouraged an exodus from the island, and among those who left was the young scholar and painter.

The earliest known document relating to him, the letter from Giulio Clovio dated 1570, refers to him as a pupil of Titian's. It was natural for a Cretan to make for Venice, for the island was a Venetian dominion. At that time the city was the new home of thousands of 'Greeks' from the Venetian territories of the eastern Mediterranean, and the presence of so many 'Grechi' in the city adds to the difficulty of tracing reference to one individual: Domenicos Theotocopoulos now becomes simply 'il Greco'.

The time of the young Domenicos' removal to Venice could not have been more favourable. It was the time of the apogee of Venetian painting, when Titian, Tintoretto and Veronese were all working in the city. It must have been an immense inspiration to work with the great master of colour. Titian was in his eighties and working in his last grand manner, and on the death in 1564 in Rome of Michelangelo, his only peer, he was the greatest living artist. The year 1564 was possibly not far from the date when El Greco entered his studio.

Perhaps he had the added inspiration of aiding Titian in his important commissions

1. *Saint John the Baptist in the Wilderness* (with a view of The Escorial). Oil on canvas. 43¾ × 26 in. (111 × 66 cm.). Signed. *c.* 1600. M.H. de Young Memorial Museum, San Francisco.

2. *Saint Jerome as Cardinal*. Oil on canvas.
43⅝ × 37⅝ in. (111 × 96 cm.). Signed. *c.* 1600.
The Frick Collection, New York.

3. *Cardinal Juan de Tavera*. Oil on canvas.
40½ × 32¼ in. (103 × 82 cm.). *c.* 1610.
Hospital de Tavera (Hospital de San Juan
Bautista), Toledo.

4. *Saint Paul* (holding an Epistle addressed to Titus, first Bishop of the Cretans). Oil on canvas. 38×30½ in. (96×77 cm.). Signed. *c.* 1610. Museo del Greco, Toledo.

5. *View and Plan of Toledo*. Oil on canvas. 59×90 in. (132×228 cm.). *c.* 1610. Museo del Greco, Toledo.

6. *The Adoration of the Shepherds*
(with the artist as the figure kneeling
before the Virgin). Oil on canvas.
126 × 70⅜ in. (320 × 180 cm.).
1612—14. Museo del Prado, Madrid.

for Philip II of Spain, for in 1567 the master refers to a young pupil assisting him on the *Martyrdom of Saint Lawrence*, the great masterpiece of his last years destined for the Escorial. At this time El Greco would have heard of the Spanish King's vast project of the Escorial, the monastery and palace which had begun building in 1563, from which the King was to direct his great crusade for the Faith — directed against the heretic at home, the Infidel in the Mediterranean, and towards the conversion of the heathen in the Indies; for the King was seeking painters to decorate his great enterprise. His first feelings of sympathy for the Spanish spirit probably originated at this time: Spain too had been close to the Orient, and had not completely broken with the medieval world, and she could appear at this moment as the one real champion of the Faith. It was to be a long time, however, before he moved to Spain.

He had entered a new world, and was confronted with an infinity of new impressions which he eagerly sought to understand. The ideas and meaning of this new world were as important to the young scholar and painter as their expression in painting. Among the painters he looked to for inspiration, Titian was, if the most important, by no means the only one, and the nature of El Greco's studies in Venice indicates a strong personality with a sense of his own special gifts. He seems to have arrived with no preconceived respect for the authority of an established style or personality, or indeed for the new culture. His attitude, however, implies not disrespect, but a desire to comprehend his new environment. His works in Venice show him trying out the new subject-matter, its new interpretation, and the new techniques.

He was by no means a great artist in Venice. The *Modena Triptych* (Plate i) the earliest work known, could easily be by any one of a number of provincial 'Greek' artists working in the city. It is a work that unfortunately tells us nothing of his painting in Crete. Painted probably not long after his arrival in Venice, there is nothing in it that is transitional. For the flat and relatively rigid geometrical designs of Byzantine art he has substituted the looser, more naturalistic and three-dimensional designs of Italian and Venetian inspirations. The compositions are not original, being borrowed from a variety of sources probably through engravings. The art of engraving had developed considerably in the first half of the sixteenth century and was of inestimable value to a young artist seeking to acquaint himself with the achievements of European art.

The remaining few paintings bear witness to the broad source of his inspiration. He made his own the freedom of the Venetian 'open' technique, of which his master was the supreme exponent. He essays Tintoretto's style, with its employment of space and movement as dramatic elements of the design (Plate iii). Later, in his efforts to express another reality, that of the spirit, he was to throw aside those dramatic empty spaces and violent perspectives; movement, however, was to remain an essential part of his painting. Similarly, he introduces himself to the possibilities of light as a dramatic element in design, especially perhaps by reference to Bassano; but the naturalism and rustic atmosphere of the Venetian's paintings he found irrelevant, as indeed he could feel little sympathy generally for the Renaissance Italian concession to a human, temporal or local interpretation of the universal and spiritual.

There was little that he did not try out in Venice, and little specifically hecould make his own. Nevertheless, it was in Venice that he was introduced to a free technique, to a painting that believed in the primacy of colour, and to the dramatic possibilities of light and movement, that is, to the essential bases of his technique.

'There has just arrived in Rome a young painter . . .' (Giulio Clovio, letter to Cardinal Farnese, 1570.)

In 1570, the first certain date in El Greco's biography, he moves to Rome, the capital of the Christian world, and the great artistic centre of Italy, where Michelangelo had only recently died. It was there that he was to complete his artistic training and his introduction to the new ideas of the West.

Giulio Clovio, a 'Greek' from Croatia, introduces the young Cretan to Cardinal Alessandro Farnese, to whom he was artistic adviser and in whose famous library he was employed as a miniaturist. We do not know El Greco's self-portrait that Clovio so highly extolled, but his report probably shows some over-enthusiasm for his young friend. El Greco does, indeed, prove himself an able follower of Titian in the portrait of Giulio Clovio (Plate iv), probably painted soon after his arrival in Rome, but there is little anticipation of the individual quality of his later works which made him one of the few really great portrait painters of all time.

His introduction to the Cardinal did lead to some patronage, although he does not appear to have received any important commissions in Rome, nor does it seem that the 'young' artist who stayed in the Farnese Palace — he was apparently nearly thirty years of age when he arrived in Rome — had any need to seek commissions for his livelihood. In fact, almost all his paintings in Italy were very small, many of them almost miniatures, and only in Rome are there two or three portraits and one or two compositions of less modest size. What was of consequence to him was his introduction to the circle of scholars and men of religion who frequented the Farnese Library, and also the new impressions of the formal art of Rome.

If El Greco's attitude when he first arrived in Italy was remarkable, his almost naive integrity was even more startling in Rome. The memory of Michelangelo was almost sacred, and had produced something of an artistic tyranny in the city, where nobody could easily question the learned and inhibiting theory that purported to understand and give authority to his style. If the style it encouraged was appropriate to the frigid and correct exposition of dogma, one of the consequences of the deliberations of Trent, it had little to recommend itself to El Greco. He questioned the very basis of its ideal figure art, with its insistence on the primacy of form and drawing, to which colour was a mere adjunct. He could have had even less sympathy for the importance attached to the study of anatomy by contemporary artists in Rome. Similarly the construction of space according to mathematical rules of perspective, although employed in an irrational way by the Roman Mannerists, meant little to him.

Nevertheless, as in Venice, he was able to profit greatly from his stay in the Holy City. Above all, he could derive much from the spirit, if not the letter, of the High Renaissance, especially from Raphael and the early Michelangelo, and his paintings in Rome gain in largeness of conception (Plate v). He was also possibly the only artist of his time to appreciate Michelangelo's late style. If Venice had introduced him to so much that was important, Michelangelo's inspired and individual treatment of form in his last years indicated to El Greco the infinite possibilities of the more flexible technique of painting. The small *Pietà* (Plate vi) is a direct interpretation in paint of Michelangelo's late sculptured group now in Florence Cathedral, and then in Rome.

In the group of portraits in the *Christ driving the Traders from the Temple* (Plate v), he acknowledges his debt to Michelangelo and Titian, and possibly also to Raphael. The painting, first composed in Venice, loses much of its loose, disturbed quality, by contact with Rome. In his compositions in Rome and his first years in Spain, he employs figures directly inspired by the heroic style of Michelangelo (especially Plates viii, xii and xiii). Later, they were to go, once he was able to replace them by his own.

Contemporary Roman Mannerist painting was also not without its fruitful influence: the vertical compositions and shallow construction of space pointed the way to the elimination of three-dimensional space (especially Plate xiii); and the combination of the more vivid and less natural colour of Rome with the richer, more substantial colour of Venice helped to lay the basis of his own personal and dramatic use of colour.

It is clear that he had very little in common with the painters of Rome. Neither could he be entirely in sympathy with the Humanist atmosphere of the Papal City: the 'divine' of Michelangelo was a reference to the gods of pagan mythology, as the conception of the heroic was derived from the spirit of ancient history and myth. El Greco's prototype of the great artist was to be Saint Luke; his prototype of the heroic, the great martyrs of the Faith. To El Greco, the Roman brand of Humanism celebrated the greatness of Man — of the individual — on account of his material potentialities; El Greco, from medieval Crete, believed in the importance of Man on account of his unique spiritual being, through which, alone, the meaning of the Universe could be fulfilled. His discussions with the Spanish Humanists in the Farnese Library would have indicated an attitude in Spain — where it was possible for the great Gothic cathedrals of Salamanca and Segovia to be erected at the same time as the Escorial — closer to his own, and it was from them that he received his first important commission, and the opportunity to go to Spain. The news, received in Rome in 1571, of the great victory over the Turk at Lepanto, off the Greek mainland, must have encouraged some sympathy in the Greek artist for Spain's crusade, as later it was to inspire his *Adoration of the Name of Jesus* (Plate xii).

It is unnecessary to believe that he was forced to leave Rome on account of the hostility of the artists caused by his presumption in offering to paint a 'Last Judgment' not inferior to Michelangelo's, if the work were pulled down, as related by Mancini some half a century later. At the time that El Greco was in Rome there were proposals to cover up the 'indecent' parts of Michelangelo's great work in the Sistine Chapel, composed entirely of nude figures, and Mancini no doubt merely relates a rumour, which however, certainly reflects something of El Greco's attitude.

Rome was unpropitious to his genius. In 1576 he received the offer of an important commission for Toledo, made by the Dean of Toledo Cathedral through the agency of his brother in Rome, and he accepted — surely with the hope eventually of working for the Escorial.

'*To express my gratitude, I agree to accept 1000 ducados instead of the 1500 offered . . .*' (El Greco, in the agreement for his first commission in Spain, 1577.)

Certainly the Dean's brother must have given a good account of the painter, for immediately on his arrival in Toledo and before starting the work for the church of Santo Domingo he was commissioned to paint the *Espolio* for the Cathedral. For the first time he had been given the opportunity to paint on a monumental scale. To express his pleasure at seeing the fulfilment of his ambition so near he offered to accept the small sum of 1000 *ducados* instead of the 1500 offered for the work for Santo Domingo, which involved the designing of the whole scheme of decoration. The two commissions were to occupy him fully for two years, and their importance inspired him to produce a whole series of masterpieces (Plates vii-x).

He was now thirty-five years of age. In Italy, he had completed his artistic training, and he no longer needed to look to art for his inspiration. The first real application of the lessons learnt was not until he arrived in Spain, and his painting really began with these two commissions.

Each painting was treated as a separate problem, as indeed later each subject was to decide its own appropriate colour, light, pattern and rhythm. In the first work, the *Assumption*, he seeks to treat in his own way a composition finally of Venetian inspiration; in the second, the *Trinity*, it is a composition essentially inspired by Michelangelo, and a grand development of his own *Pietà* painted in Rome. In the *Adoration of the Shepherds*, the problem is especially that of light; and in the *Resurrection*, dramatic movement, and a more supernatural light. The *Saint John the Evangelist* attempts to express the heroic in his own way; and the majestic Christ of the *Espolio* is the first of his completely personal images, in which pattern, movement and colour, type and gesture are in complete harmony, and in accord with the one expression. This painting is also the one of greatest variety and vitality in the handling.

In all these paintings, he begins to develop his own expressive colour. Colour and light begin to combine, and take on a quality of flux. Space is little more than implied, and the distinction between sky and earth goes: the motifs of the open tomb of the *Assumption*, the rocks of the *Resurrection* and the ground of the *Espolio*, do not disturb the essential verticality of the compositions. The figures have lost much of their corporeality, but not their grandeur, by their surface treatment in colour and light. In this development, the nude figure of Christ of the *Trinity*, inspired by Michelangelo's heroic figure style, is the least advanced, and the single draped figure of *Saint John the Evangelist*, the most advanced. Draperies are indeed at this stage treated more freely than the figures, and become an expressive element in themselves. Both shade and light are active in colour, and if they still imply modelling of the forms, they do not stress the quality of relief.

Each composition is inspired by its appropriate movement: the grand slow tempo of the soaring image of the Virgin of the *Assumption*; the urgent and arrested rhythm of the shepherds of the *Adoration*; and above all the tremendous contained movement of the Christ of the *Espolio*. Movement was to be an essential element of his painting.

All the paintings are full of reminiscences of Italy, and it is some few years before they disappear. He has, however, started on the path he was to follow to its conclusion, and the advance made during the two years was immense. If he were to express the spiritual, it would be by other than material means, and the process of dematerialisation has begun. Neither corporeality, nor a distinction between earth and sky, belonged to the realm of the spirit; neither could the ideal figure art of Rome with its pagan implications, nor the sensual art of Venice with its temporal concessions, be reconciled to the expression of his view of the essential spiritual meaning of the Universe. He now sought to create a painting from colour and light, pattern and movement, and without any direct reference to the art of the past or present.

His unyielding attitude before interference with his artistic interpretation of a subject is brought out in the arguments over the valuation of the *Espolio*; El Greco ignored the demands made by the Cathedral authorities — probably largely to support a low valuation — to make certain drastic changes to his painting. The remarks of El Greco's valuers, when he finally agreed to accept about a third of the previous valuation, that if the painting should be valued at its true worth, there would be few or none prepared to pay', express the startling impression made on the artists in Toledo by El Greco's first works.

Shortly after he arrived in Toledo he must have made acquaintance with a Spanish lady, Jerónima de las Cuevas, who became his life-long companion, and who in 1578 gave him a son, Jorge Manuel, to whom he became a devoted father. All we know of the lady whom he never married is the sympathetic portrait painted apparently at the beginning of their acquaintance (Plate xi). He introduces us to his son on a number of occassions (Plates xvii, xxxvi and xxxviii).

'*His painting did not please the King . . .*' (Sigüenza, History of the Jeronymite Order, 1608.)

El Greco was recognised as an artist of outstanding merit, and he had met with sympathetic patrons. In 1579, immediately after the conclusion of his first commissions for Toledo, the long-desired opportunity to work for the Escorial was offered him. He had already painted the *Adoration of the Name of Jesus* (Plate xii) for the King, and he was now invited to paint specifically for the Escorial. Navarrete had died, and Philip II was looking for someone to replace the painter he so admired. El Greco put everything into the painting, the *Martyrdom of Saint Maurice and his Legions* (Plate xiii), and produced a work of astounding power and originality. Already in the *Espolio*, he had daringly introduced the grand passage of vivid red in the mantle of Christ; in the *Saint Maurice*, an intense blue animates the whole composition. The complementary strident yellow enhances the powerful and moving impression. Before he started to paint the picture he had already decided on the colour that would best symbolise the event, and this becomes an essential consideration in all his subsequent painting.

He worked for two years on the painting: if he were successful, his great ambition would be fulfilled. But he was to be disappointed. The splendid masterpiece of painting did not please the King, who commissioned another artist to make a substitute.

14

El Greco turned to his first patrons in Toledo, and he was not given another opportunity to work for the King.

It was perhaps inevitable, and, in the event, it was fortunate. His genius was too independent to serve the austere and rigid demands of the Escorial. His art, also, was not concerned with the militant aspect of religion, in which the Inquisition and its *autos-da-fé* played so important a part in Spain at that time. But in Toledo, the great cultural and ecclesiastical centre of Spain, he was to find a sympathetic atmosphere, a select circle of friends among the men of religion, scholars and poets of the town, and an appreciative and loyal clientele. The poets Góngora and Paravicino were among his friends; the great mystics Saint Teresa of Jesus and Saint John of the Cross visited the town. It was a time in Spain of great religious fervour and spiritual activity — possibly found in its most concentrated form in Toledo — which reached its climax in the years El Greco was in the town.

'*The citizens of Toledo never tire of seeing his painting . . .*' (Alonso de Villegas, *Flos Sanctorum*, 1588.)

The failure at the Escorial closed five years of uninterrupted activity in Spain. There followed a few years of respite before any comparable commissions came his way. For El Greco this was a period of reflection, the outcome of which was the final declaration of his aesthetic. If his efforts before were particularly directed towards preparation for the Escorial, his time was now employed in getting to know more intimately the atmosphere of Toledo, in meeting with kindred spirits, and in coming to terms with himself. He finally succeeds in eliminating all direct references to the art of Venice and Rome, and the process of dematerialisation is continued.

To this period belong the *Saint Mary Magdalene* (Plate xv), which still reveals its Venetian, specifically Titianesque, inspiration, and the *Saint Sebastian* (Plate xiv) whose Roman derivation is still apparent. At this time too he painted the *Immaculate Conception* (Plate xvi), in which for the first time there is a clear recollection of his early impressions of Byzantine art. These are however among the last paintings to make any clear references to the art of Byzantium, Venice or Rome.

His first completely personal work, the *Burial of the Count of Orgaz* (Plate xvii), was painted in 1586, when he was forty-five. In this painting any description of space, or of the corporeality of the figures, has completely gone, allowing an undisturbed expression of the spiritual atmosphere of the scene, and of the spiritual or psychological presence of the participants. To El Greco there could not be the easy concession of depicting Heaven and Earth as two separate things, physically distinct as the earth and sky. To him, as to a Saint Teresa of Jesus, the spiritual was omnipresent: present in the celestial visitors who lay the body to rest, and expressed in the remarkable pattern formed by the two Saints and in the colour of their vestments; present in the souls of men, and realised in the activity of the earthly participants 'in the miraculous event; pervading the whole scene, and expressed in the variety, splendour and activity of the colour and light. And the spiritual was the only significant reality.

There is absolutely no confusion, but a grand equilibrium, yet movement is an essential part of the expression: the composition, shapes, gestures, colour and light are made active and living symbols. These separate elements, and the particular rhythm that informs them, derive from the meaning of the supernatural image or event. Henceforth, El Greco was to express the spiritual by strictly extra-natural means, and the development of his paintings was in the direction of a greater simplification of the means and a greater concentration of the expression.

If the popular success of the *Burial of the Count of Orgaz* depended largely on the 'life-like portrayal of men of Toledo of his time', he had become, for his life-time at least, an almost legendary figure to Toledans.

After the completion of the painting some ten years were to elapse before, in 1596, he was again given any comparable commissions. It was nevertheless a period of great activity, in which he was engaged on a host of smaller commissions. In this decade he formulated his repertoire of subjects and worked out their individual interpretation.

Painting in Spain in the sixteenth century, still partly medieval in character, was almost totally confined to religious subjects, and especially concerned itself with the devotional image. El Greco was in sympathy with this. He did not so much extend the range of subjects as revivify them, giving meaning and reality to the images.

The Old Testament does not figure in his repertoire of subjects, which concerns itself with the central personalities and mysteries of the Faith, in which were embodied the essential meaning of the Universe. The mysteries were those which expressed the essence of the spiritual, essentially divorced from ordinary human experience: the Virgin of the Annunciation (Plates xx and xxxiv) receiving the Spirit, and the Christ on the Cross releasing the Spirit (Plates xxiii and xxxv); the Christ of His Mystic Birth (Plate xxi and Fig. 6) and of the Resurrection (Plates ix and xxiv); the Christ of the Baptism (Plate xxii) and the Pentecost (Plate xxv), both themes of the descent of the Spirit. These six subjects he composed together in the grand unified programme dedicated to the 'life of Christ', for the Colegio de Doña María in Madrid (Plates xx to xxv). It is clear he must have played an important part in the devising of the programme, and certainly in its interpretation.

16

In his interpretation of these subjects, the grand poetry of the Holy Scriptures was an integral and essential part of the mystery, and it is expressed in the setting as in the whole pictorial conception. The apocalyptical character of his painting increases, and it is appropriate that two of his last works were the *Immaculate Conception* (Plate xvi) the great masterpiece of his last years, and a subject of purely supernatural implication, which he related to Saint John's vision of the Apocalypse, and Saint John's *Vision of the Opening of the Fifth Seal* (Plate xlviii), in both of which he supremely realises the tremendous visionary poetry of the Revelations.

An important place in his repertoire of subjects was taken by the image of Christ, the Virgin and the Saints near to Christ. These images were of two types. The one is the simple image of the Saint, in which he sought to express by a characteristic type and gesture, and by pattern, colour and movement, the essence of the personality and its meaning. To this category belong the series of *Apostolados*, in which Christ and the Apostles appear as separate images (Fig. 4), and the *Saints Francis and Andrew* (Plate xix), *Saint Bernardino* (Plate xxxvii), and the late *Saint Peter* (Plate xlv), possibly the grandest of all. The other type is that of the Saint in ecstasy or inspired, and related to some specific and characteristic situation. Of this type are the penitent *Saint Mary Magdalene* (Plate xv is an early painting), *Saint Jerome* (Plate xlvi), the *Saint Francis receiving the Stigmata*, and the *Saint Ildefonso* inspired writing his dissertation on the Purity of the Virgin (Plate xli). The two last Saints are unexpected in his repertoire, which otherwise confines itself to the New Testament, but their presence can be explained by the closeness to Christ of Saint Francis who receives the Stigmata — there is little of the human, 'gentle' Saint — and the fact that Saint Ildefonso was the patron Saint and the first Bishop of Toledo.

The idea of the pairs of Saints which appear at this time was not his own, and he would have known the great series painted by Navarrete for the Escorial. El Greco introduces them into his repertoire in the 1590s, and the juxtaposition of two different personalities in the one painting was an invaluable exercise in bringing out the character of each. Saint Peter and Saint Paul, the two Saint Johns, were obvious pairs, but he also brings together such diverse characters as the *Saint Andrew and Saint Francis* (Plate xix).

'*Toledo was more propitious to his genius . . .*' (Paravicino, on the death of El Greco, 1614.) Paravicino in his sonnet dedicated to his friend recognises the great significance of the atmosphere of Toledo to the great painter, and El Greco confesses his debt to the town by introducing into his paintings the landscape of Toledo, as earlier in Italy he had introduced the portraits of the great painters of Venice and Rome. The view of Toledo first appears in the *Saint Joseph and the Christ Child* (Plate xxvi), painted in 1597, the year which marks the beginning of a whole series of important commissions which keep him occupied until his death in 1614. In this painting, whose theme is that of Man cherishing the spiritual meaning of the Universe and guided by it in his path through the World, the spiritual view of Toledo seems to symbolise the World. The Metropolitan Museum painting (Plate xxix) was probably conceived in connection with the same commission, for the view is the same, and the result was one of the most remarkable independent landscapes ever painted. The town appears subsequently in a number of paintings, where its presence is appropriate: in the *Christ on the Cross* leaving this World (Plate xxxv); and in the late *Immaculate Conception* (Plate xliii), where it is little more than a vision. Significantly, in the *Saint John the Baptist in the Wilderness* (Fig. 1), the setting is the austere landscape of the Escorial. Although he had visited the Escorial in his first years in Spain, the studies for this landscape, like those of Toledo, were almost certainly made around 1596, when he visited Madrid in connection with the commission for the Colegio de Doña María. While the views keep close to the actual features of the landscapes, they are given a completely spiritual interpretation. The same thing occurs in his portraits.

The years 1600 to 1610 witnessed the full development of his powers as a portrait painter (Plates xxxii, xxxvi and xlii). His personal style of portrait painting begins with the *Burial of the Count of Orgaz*, and closes with his great masterpiece, the portrait of his friend *Paravicino* (Plate xlii), painted in 1609 or 1610. Essentially related to the development of his portrait art was his great exercise in interpreting the characters of the Saints. In both he sought to express the reality of the spiritual personality.

'I have applied observations made of celestial bodies . . .' (El Greco, inscription on his *View and Plan of Toledo, c.* 1610.)
Toward the end of his life, the supernatural takes over. The late *Immaculate Conception* (Plate xliii) is not so much an expression of the mystery as its realisation in painting. A parallel expression is found only in the mystic poets of his time:

'On a Night dark and unfathomable, as anguish was consumed in flames of Love . . . I left my house, tranquil and calm, unseen and I not seeing, without any guide but the light that burned in my heart, . . . more resplendent than the Noon . . .
In his 'Songs of the Soul', Saint John of the Cross, El Greco's almost exact contemporary, expresses the same infinity of spiritual space, in which an all-resplendent light and an infinite darkness are compatibles.

18

The towering, rock-like form of *Saint Peter* (Plate xlv), and the ecstatic *Visitation* (Plate xliv), with its strange impression of the 'coming together of two celestial bodies in space' (Camón-Aznar, *Dominico Greco*, 1950), belong to the same commission as the *Immaculate Conception*. His *Penitent Saint Jerome* (Plate xlvi) is a purely spiritual presence, whose material being is dissolved in the impassioned handling. The tremendous vision of *Saint John* (Plate xlviii) belongs to his last unfinished commission for the Hospital de San Juan Bautista, Toledo, and this vision of the Apocalypse fitly closes his career.

'Michelangelo was a good man, but he could not paint . . .' (Pacheco, 'Arte de la Pintura', referring to the year 1611.)

It was in 1611 that Pacheco visited El Greco in Toledo. The erudite Sevillian painter was collecting material for his 'Book of Portraits' of eminent men and his 'Art of Painting', and made the journey to meet the great painter of Toledo whose fame had reached Seville. The Sevillian gives an honest and discerning report, in which admiration and understanding are mixed with a certain perplexity. It is the only contemporary account of El Greco's personality, ideas and methods of painting — apart from the eulogies of Góngora and Paravicino. Pacheco's learned theories, if not his real sympathies, sought to uphold the primacy of Italian Renaissance painting, whose one exemplar was Michelangelo. He asks El Greco his opinion of Michelangelo as a painter, and El Greco shrewdly replies that he was not a painter, but that he was 'a good man'. This was one 'discerning remark' not appreciated by Pacheco, who was however not too surprised, for Domenicos was 'singular in everything'. There is, indeed, a truth in El Greco's reply: Michelangelo was essentially the great sculptor of the century, concerned with the human figure, form and drawing: El Greco was the great painter of the century, concerned with colour, whose art had less in common with that of the great Italian master than with that of the great contemporary poets and mystics, Paravicino and Góngora, Saint John of the Cross and Saint Teresa of Jesus. There is, however, a remarkable consonance between the late endeavours of Michelangelo as a sculptor and El Greco as a painter, each of whom exploited to the limits the expressive possibilities of their respective materials — form and colour.

Pacheco watched El Greco paint, and describes for us his 'open' and flexible technique; his diligence in making small-scale preparatory paintings; how he began with painting the design in red or black chiaroscuro — not a drawing, but the first broad statement of the design and movement in tone. The more general and 'certain' course was to make a precise delineation of the forms, and then 'fill in' with the 'final colours'.

El Greco's method included no drawing or filling in, but was essentially the heightening of the first broad preliminary painting by superimposing passages and touches of colour, until he had given a final variety and effectiveness to the colours, and vitality to the design. It was the last essential touches, those 'sketchy brushstrokes made to affect dexterity', that Pacheco was unable to understand. His infinitely flexible technique, including the use of superimposed glazes of colour as well as touches of pure paint, sought to give that living quality to his paintings, observed by Góngora: 'His brush gave life and soul to the canvas.'

'His rare distinction, Ages will admire, not imitate . . .' (Paravicino, sonnet dedicated to El Greco, 1614.)

Like all great independent geniuses, El Greco could have no real followers. His own son was no more than a superficial imitator, who could not appreciate the essential inspiration that informed his painting. He was the one outstanding painter of his age, and no painter has better expressed the spirit of a particular time and place. He was understood by only a few in his time, and soon after his death was more or less forgotten. It is true that Velasquez and Zurbaran, who began studying painting in the 1610s, were able to find inspiration in the great Toledan's portrait and devotional art, and two hundred years later, Goya certainly paid homage to the master when he painted his *Taking of Christ* to hang next to the *Espolio* in the Sacristy of Toledo Cathedral. Delacroix the great colourist, owned one of his paintings. To the exponents of naturalism and Impressionism El Greco's art could mean little. Cézanne's copying of the portrait of Jerónima de las Cuevas appears appropriately as a herald of the recognition that was soon to follow. The first real appraisal was Cossio's work published in 1908. It is El Greco's independence and artistic integrity, and the essential freedom and painterly quality of his work that have appealed to the present century.

The resurrection of his painting in our times has encouraged attempts to make up a biography of the man. The very absence of records has encouraged a belief in his exotic character, and has allowed various misinformed explanations of his art. It is no longer necessary to consider defective vision, mental aberration or drog addiction as explanations for his painting. Neither can we know him better by seeking to put an intriguing interpretation on his relationship with Doña Jerónima. The fact is, we know practically nothing about the man: time has preserved for us only the splendid revelations of one of the greatest and most individual masters of colour.

Outline Biography of El Greco

1540/1541 Domenicos Theotocopoulos born in Candia, Crete in 1541 or the end of 1540. The only evidence for the date of birth is the artist's own statement, made on 31st October and again on 4th November, 1606, that he was sixty-five years of age. On two occasions, the town of Candia is specified: in Giulio Clovio's letter of 1570 and in 1582, when the artist was acting as interpreter in the trial of another 'Greek' in Toledo, when he states he was a native of the 'town of Candia'. On all other occasions, he is referred to simply as Cretan.

1560s In Venice as a pupil of Titian. Clovio's letter of 1570 is the only evidence.

End 1570 Moves from Venice to Rome. The evidence is a letter dated 16th November 1570, from Giulio Clovio in Rome addressed to Cardinal Farnese, asking the Cardinal to place the 'young Candian, a pupil of Titian's, recently arrived in Rome', under his protection and give him temporary lodging in his palace. Clovio introduces the young artist as 'in my opinion among the greatest in painting' and mentions a *Self-portrait* (lost) which 'causes wonderment among all the painters of Rome'.

1576—1577 At the end of 1576 or early in 1577, moves to Toledo, in Spain, where he finally settles.

1577 By the spring of 1577, in Toledo, to carry out the commission for Santo Domingo el Antiguo. El Greco was to paint 'all by his own hand and in Toledo'. He was also responsible for designing the retable of the main chapel with its sculptures (the Escorial artist J.B. Monegro was commissioned to carve the retable 'after the plans of Mecer Domenico Theotocopuli'). Almost all subsequent large commissions include the designing of the retables or frames for his paintings, and in some cases the sculptures. Soon after arrival in Toledo, receives the further commissions to paint the *Espolio* for the Cathedral. He had received both commissions before 2nd July 1577, the date of the earliest document establishing his presence in Toledo and Spain.

1578 Birth of a son, Jorge Manuel, to El Greco and Jerónima de las Cuevas. El Greco apparently never married.

1579 Completion of the works for Santo Domingo and the Cathedral. The *Espolio* was completed by 15th June, the date of the first valuation, and the Santo Domingo works by September. The *Espolio* valuation led to the first of a series of litigations which became a feature of almost all El Greco's important commissions. The Cathedral's valuation of roughly 225 *ducados* was answered by El Greco's of 900 *ducados*, which the Cathedral authorities considered 'beyond all reason'. An arbitrator finally valued the work at roughly 320 *ducados*, but with the observation that it was 'of the best he had ever seen' and that 'if one should value it at its true worth, it would be in a sum that few or none would be prepared to pay' — the outstanding quality of El Greco's work is acknowledged for the first time. In this litigation, the Cathedral authorities also chose to censure the artist's treatment of the subject, and stipulated that certain improprieties should be made good, 'that take authority from Christ, as the three of four heads above that of Christ, two of them with helmets; and also the Maries and our Lady are against the Gospels, for they were not in this place'. El Greco made no changes to the picture. Apparently fearful that the artist might leave Toledo with the painting, it was complained that 'he had the painting, for which he had already been paid 200 *ducados*; he was a foreigner with no property in Toledo, and had finished the work for which he came to Toledo, that is, the Santo Domingo retable, and no longer had any reason to remain.'

1579—1580 Philip II commissions the *Martyrdom of Saint Maurice and his Legions* for one of the chapels of the church of the Escorial. On 25th April 1580, the King orders the Prior of the Escorial to provide El Greco with materials, 'especially ultramarine', to enable him to carry out the commission 'made some time ago'. The painting, executed in Toledo, completed 1582. El Greco paid 800 *ducados*. The painting did not satisfy the King: 'by a Dominico Greco . . .. who paints excellent things in Toledo, is a painting of Saint Maurice and his soldiers, which he made for the altar of the Saints, and is now in the Chapter House; it did not please His Majesty, but that is not surprising, for it pleased few, although it is said it is of much art and that there are many excellent things by his hand'. (Padre Sigüenza, *Historia de la Orden de San Jerónimo*, 1608).

1585 The Dean of Toledo Cathedral commissions the retable for the *Espolio* (the retable is lost, but the carved and painted group from the retable, of the *Virgin presenting the Chasuble to Saint Ildefonso*, is still in the Cathedral).

1586 Painted the *Burial of the Count of Orgaz*. Commissioned March 1586, to be completed by Christmas of the same year. El Greco received 1200 *ducados*. A certain popular acclaim is immediately earned: 'foreigners flock to see and admire the painting, and the citizens of Toledo never tire of seeing it, as there is always something new to see, for here is portrayed, very life-like, the notable men of our time' (Alonso de Villegas, *Flos Sanctorum*, 1578). The portraits include those of himself and his son.

1591	Commission for the paintings of the high altar of the church of Talavera la Vieja, Toledo province. The paintings were: the *Coronation of the Virgin*, the model for his later versions of the same subject for the church of San José, Toledo, and the Hospital de la Caridad, Illescas; and the two full-length standing Saints, Peter and Andrew. He received 300 *ducados* for the work, which must have been largely executed by assistants.
December 1596	Commission by the Royal Council of Castile for the retable and paintings for the high altar of the Church of the Augustine College of Doña María de Aragón, Madrid, dedicated to Our Lady of the Annunciation. The College was a foundation of Doña María's, lady-in-waiting to Philip II's fourth wife (d. 1593). The paintings were executed in Toledo, and delivered July 1600; El Greco receiving nearly 6000 *ducados* for the paintings, designs for the retable, and sculptures for this large commission for the Court.
1597	November 1597, commission for the retables of the Chapel of San José, Toledo, completed two years later. El Greco received 2850 *ducados*.
1603	Contract for the *Saint Bernardino*. Paid 300 *ducados*. Contract for the Hospital de la Caridad, Illescas (between Toledo and Madrid), dated 18th June 1603. The commission given to 'Domingo Greco and Xorje Manuel, painters' (the son could hardly have been more than an assistant). The commission apparently included the decoration of the whole chapel, including the design for the retable and the provision of sculptures as well as paintings. The paintings comprised the *Virgin of Charity* and three paintings for the vault, the *Coronation of the Virgin* and the *Annunciation* and *Nativity*. The work was completed by August 1605, the date of the first valuation, which led to lengthy litigation, only finally settled in May 1607, at little more than 2000 *ducados*, actually less than the first. This time El Greco was not only censured on account of certain improprieties, but also for the poor workmanship and materials (successfully disproved). The 'improprieties' referred to the inclusion of the portraits of Jorge Manuel and other known people wearing large ruffs, and the general arrangement of the chapel, and placing of the sculptures. On El Greco's side, it was maintained that the chapel was 'the best, and in its construction, of the greatest perfection in Spain', that 'it was remarkable that the dress that all Christianity wears should be regarded as indecent' and that 'it should not be changed as otherwise they would appear as Saints instead of men'. It is not known whether El Greco ever painted over the portraits and replaced them by 'decent' figures, but it is hardly likely. At some time, however, they were overpainted, but El Greco's original figures have been recently uncovered. At one stage, the Hospital authorities threatened they would

get a painter from Madrid to paint the Virgin of Charity 'properly'.

1603—1607 In these years, Luis Tristán is recorded as a pupil of El Greco's (the only pupil of any standing).

1606 In connection with the Illescas commission, El Greco successfully contests payment of tax, arguing that he practised painting as a liberal art. This is the first occasion in Spain of official recognition of painting as a liberal, and not mechanical, art.

1607 November 1607, contract for the decoration of the Chapel of Isabel de Oballe in the Church of San Vicente, Toledo. The paintings comprised the *Immaculate Conception*, the *Visitation* for the vault, and the *Saint Peter* and *Saint Ildefonso* for the side altars. The contract stipulated that the retable was to be higher than the one designed by Semino (who had died shortly after receiving the commission), for 'to be a dwarf was the worst condition of man' — surely El Greco's remark. By August 1608, he states that the work is much advanced, but it was not completed until April 1613, a year before his death.

1608 Commissioned paintings for the church of the Hospital of San Juan Bautista (Hospital Tavera), Toledo, including the *Baptism*, finished by Jorge Manuel after his death, and the *Vision of the Apocalypse*. El Greco had been connected with the Hospital from 1595, when he received a commission for the design of a tabernacle. The Hospital, outside the walls of the town, appears on a cloud in his *View and Plan of Toledo* (Fig. 5), in the Museo del Greco, Toledo, possibly painted about this time. An inscription, composed by El Greco, on the plan of Toledo in this painting reads: '*It has been necessary to show the Hospital de Tavera as a model, for the building hides the Visagra Gate, and the dome obscures part of the town, and once treated as a model and moved from its place, it seemed better to me to show the main façade . . . the rest, and its proper relationship to the town can be seen on the plan. Also, in the representation of Our Lady presenting the Chasuble to Saint Ildefonso, in making the figures large, I have applied, in some way, the observation made of celestial bodies that an illuminated body seen at a distance may appear large although it be small*'.

1609—1610 Portrait of *Paravicino*.

1611 Visited by Pacheco. Designed a monument for the funerary celebrations in Toledo Cathedral in honour of Margarita of Austria, widow of Philip II, who had died in that year.

1612 The artist rents a family burial vault in the church of Santo Domingo el Antiguo, Toledo, the church for which he painted his first works in Spain, on condition that he builds the altar and retable at his cost. For the retable he painted the *Adoration of the Shepherds* (Fig 6), now in the Prado.

31st March 1614	El Greco 'confined to his bed', 'holding, believing and confessing the Faith of the Holy Church of Rome... in whose Faith I have lived and die, as a faithful and Catholic Christian ... because of the gravity of my sickness I was unable to make a will', gives power to Jorge Manuel Teotocopuli 'my son and of Doña Jerónima de las Cuevas, who is a person of honesty and virtue', to make his testament, arrange his burial, and pay his debts, and the 'remainder of my possessions to go to Jorge Manuel, as universal heir ...'
7th April 1614	El Greco dies.—'dominico greco, On the seventh (of April) dominico greco died, made no will. Received the sacraments, was buried in Sto domingo el antiguo, gave mass' (entry in Book of Burials of the parish of Santo Tomé, Toledo).
7th July 1614	The inventory of El Greco's possessions made by his son included the following items in his studio: 143 paintings, mostly finished, a few merely primed canvasses, some painted as far as the chiaroscuro design, and some 'unfinished'; 30 models in clay and wax and 15 in plaster; 27 books in the Greek language, including the philosophers and poets, Old and New Testaments, and the Fathers of the Church; 67 books in Italian, and 17 in Spanish. 120 drawings (probably the larger part his own, but unfortunately only three or four certain drawings have come down to us); 30 plans (probably for retables); and 200 engravings (a collection of engravings for reference and study was part of any artist's studio).

Further dates relating to El Greco's career

1563	Building of El Escorial commenced.
1564	Death of Michelangelo in Rome.
1571	Victory of Lepanto.
1576	Death of Titian in Venice.
1579	The body of Don Juan de Austria (d. 1578), victor of Lepanto, translated to the Pantheon of the Escorial.
1579	Death of the Spanish painter Navarrete, leaving unfinished the greater part of the commission to provide paintings for the thirty-six chapels of the church of the Escorial.
1582	Death of Saint Teresa of Jesus.
1584	Death of the Spanish painter, Luis de Morales, 'el Divino'.
1591	Death of Saint John of the Cross.
1598	Death of Philip II.
1599	Birth of Velasquez.

Pacheco on El Greco

The few passages in Pacheco's 'Arte de la Pintura' contain the only comments on the man and his painting made by a contemporary acquaintance, with the exception of the eulogies of Paravicino and Góngora, and the text is given in full: 'The most important part of painting is "relief", and there are many great painters who have possessed this quality alone, as Bassano, Caravaggio and our Ribera, and we may also include Domenico Greco, for although I have disagreed with certain of his opinions and paradoxes, it is not possible to exclude him from the number of great painters, for I have seen some works by him of such "relief" and so alive — in his particular manner — that they rank with the greatest' (Book 2, chapter 10).

'Among the exponents of this manner (referring to the Venetian "open" technique) there have been great painters, including especially Bassano, whose sketches are superior to many finished works by others: and in Spain there has been one who has endeavoured to give distinction to an individual kind of "sketch", not practised before and not followed since' (Book 2, chapter 11, Sánchez Cantón properly considers this to be a reference to El Greco).

Pacheco refers to the various ways of carrying out a painting after the initial drawing has been made on the canvas: 'Some start their painting by using only black and white . . . or red and white' (that is, monochrome under-painting) '. . . some paint directly using the final colours . . . the advantage of oil is that one can retouch . . . as Titian. Some when they have finished the underpainting, complete the work by adding final rapid strokes (*'borrones'*) intending thereby to demonstrate greater facility and dexterity than others. And who would believe that Domenico Greco retouched his paintings many times in order to keep the colours separate and distinct, and added those violent brushstrokes to affect mastery . . . this I call working to be poor.'

Pacheco continues by recommending that the flesh parts be painted first, and that finally one should go over the painting and give it 'finish'. It is understandable that he was a little perplexed by El Greco's completely different method of painting (Book 3, chapter 5).

'In our time, there have been painters learned not only in their profession but also in the humanities, as Michelangelo, also a poet; Leonardo da Vinci . . . ; Vasari; and Domenico Greco, who was a great philosopher, shrewd in his remarks, and wrote on painting, sculpture and architecture' (Book 3, chapter 9).

'This honour (of being the great painter of Saint Francis) belongs to El Greco, for he conformed most closely to the story' (additions, concerning the proper treatment of religious subjects).

Pacheco discussed the importance of drawing: 'I was thus amazed on asking El Greco in 1611 which was the more important, drawing or colouring, that he should say colouring, but this was not so surprising as to hear him speak with so little respect of Michelangelo, "the Father of Painting", saying that he was a good man but that he did not know how to paint. It will not, however, surprise those who know him, that he should depart from the generally held opinion, for in everything, as in painting, he was singular' (Book 2, chapter 5).

Pacheco refers to El Greco's individual opinion, in opposition to that of Aristotle and of the antique authors, that the painter does not necessarily have to follow certain prescribed rules (Book 12, chapter 12).

Góngora and Paravicino on El Greco

'This hard stone, of shining porphyry and elegant form, denies to the world the softest brush ever to give soul to panel, life to canvas. Oh traveller! Honour it, and go on your way! Here lies the Greek. Nature inherits Art; ...; Iris, Colour; Phoebus, Light; though Morpheus his shades are not augmented ...'. (Góngora, Sonnet, 'A funeral lament to El Greco', 1614).

'Of El Greco that which can be confined lies at rest ... His fame, Earth will not suffer obscure, yet Envy seeks ... He worked, a greater Apelles in a greater Age; applause was his, not sought; his rare distinction Ages will admire, not imitate. Crete gave him his life, and brushes; Toledo, a better land, where he begins with Death to attain, Eternity.' (Paravicino, Sonnet, 'A funeral lament to El Greco, 1614).

Notes on the Plates

Plate i *The Modena Triptych.* Tempera on panel. The side panels each 9⅝ × 7 in. (24.5 × 18 cm.); the triptych closed, including the frame, 14½ × 9⅜ in. (37 × 23.8 cm.). Signed. 1560 – 65. Galleria Estense, Modena.

Small portable altarpiece with hinged wings, painted on both sides, of a type similar in form to others produced in Crete in the sixteenth century, but with an Italian Renaissance frame. The subjects on the front, from left to right, are the *Adoration of the Shepherds*, the *Allegory of a Christian Knight*, and the *Baptism*; and on the back, the *Annunciation, Mount Sinai*, and *Adam and Eve*. The central panel, showing the Christian Knight received into Heaven, with Purgatory and Inferno below, and the three Theological virtues, is of medieval inspiration, and precisely follows a known representation of the subject. The Jaws of Hell are a specifically medieval motif. Saint Catherine, with the Wheel of her Martyrdom, appears below the figures of Christ and the Knight. The theme of Mount Sinai, on the back of the central panel, was of Cretan origin, and faithfully repeats a traditional Byzantine model. The picture shows pilgrims on the way to the Monastery, and the Mountain as the Road to Heaven. The reference to Saint Catherine in both the central panels has been suggested as a possible indication of the artist's connection in Crete with the monastery of Saint Catherine, a dependency of that of Mount Sinai, and the most important school of painting in the island. The other compositions are similarly not original, but here the artist has used engravings after Italian (mainly Venetian) compositions as his models. The repetition of traditional images was usual in Byzantine art. The Triptych is interesting as the earliest known work by El Greco. It clearly belongs to the time soon after his arrival in Italy. We see the artist acquainting himself with the new Italian subject matter and its treatment, and making his first essays in the new technique of Venice. The flat, linear, geometrical designs of Byzantine art give way to compositions employing rounder, more solid forms, and a looser handling. The somewhat nervous quality may be regarded as El Greco's own, and the Triptych does contain motifs and compositions that he later develops. The subjects of the *Annunciation, Adoration of the Shepherds* and *Baptism* inspire some of El Greco's grandest works (Plates xx, xxi, and xxii). *The Allegory of the Christian Knight* is appropriately recollected in the *Allegory of the Holy League* (Plate xii). The Byzantine image of *Mount Sinai* is not unreasonably brought to mind in front of the late *Toledo* (Plate xxix).

Plate ii *Mount Sinai.* The back of the central panel of the *Modena Triptych* (see preceding note).

Plate iii *Christ healing the Blind.* Oil on canvas. 19¾ × 24 in. (50 × 61 cm.). Signed. *c.* 1570. Pinacoteca, Parma.

Possibly the sequel to the *Christ driving the Traders from the Temple* (Matthew, XXI, 14: 'And the blind and the lame came to him in the temple; and he healed them'). Both subjects were treated by El Greco more than once in Italy. This is the smallest known painting on canvas by El Greco. The painting has been cut and the group on the right is incomplete. No large-scale works are known from his Italian period, and most are quite small. He does not appear to have received any important commissions before he moved to Spain. Three versions of this subject are known, all basically the same in composition, but differing in treatment. The earliest, an unsigned panel in Dresden, is looser in composition, smaller in conception, and introduces *genre* motifs of a dog, sack and pitcher in the foreground, eliminated in subsequent versions. The present painting, probably also painted in Venice, is more easily composed. The third and largest painting, now in a private collection in New York (possibly identical with the one in a Madrid collection at the time of Cossío's pioneer work on El Greco), with its comparative largeness of conception, belongs to his Roman period, after 1570. El Greco did not again take up the subject in Spain. The inspiration is from

28

Venice. The dramatic use of recession behind the figures in the foreground is Tintoretto's invention. El Greco is still borrowing certain motifs, but the composition would seem to be original. The painting was among the Farnese possessions in the seventeenth century, and was probably brought to Rome by the artist, unless it was painted soon after his arrival in 1570. The figure on the extreme left, looking out towards the spectator, is certainly the young El Greco. He appears, however, nearer twenty than thirty years old.

Plate iv *Portrait of Giulio Clovio*. Oil on canvas. 25 × 34½ in. (63 × 88.5 cm.). Signed. *c.* 1571. Museo di Capodimonte, Naples.

Giulio Clovio (1498 – 1578), a 'Greek' from Croatia, friend of El Greco's, worked as a miniaturist in the Farnese Library. He is portrayed holding an open book (the *Libro della Vergine*, at the time in the Farnese Library, and now in the National Museum, Naples) displaying two of his own miniatures. The portrait was painted probably soon after El Greco arrived in Rome (November 1570), and almost certainly for his friend. In the seventeenth century, it was in the possession of Fulvio Orsini, librarian to Cardinal Farnese. This is perhaps the earliest independent portrait by the artist who was to become one of the greatest portrait painters of all time. Three splendid portraits belong to his Italian years: the present portrait, possibly the earliest, and the signed portrait of a man in Copenhagen, both Titianesque; and the more personal *Vincentio Anastagi*, a signed portrait in the Frick Collection, New York. It is unfortunate that the self-portrait mentioned by Giulio Clovio is lost.

Plate v *Christ driving the Traders from the Temple* (The Cleansing of the Temple). Oil on canvas. 46 × 59 in. (117 × 150 cm.). Signed. 1571 – 76. Institute of Arts, Minneapolis.

(Matthew, XXI, 12; the sequel is possibly the *Christ healing the Blind*.) The four portraits at the bottom right represent, from left to right, Titian, Michelangelo, Giulio Clovio and possibly El Greco himself. The introduction of Titian and Michelangelo is clearly an acknowledgment of his debt to these two artists. To his friend, Giulio Clovio, he owed his introduction to the Farnese household. The young man looking out, pointing to himself, has similar features to the self-portrait in the *Christ healing the Blind* at Parma (Plate iii), but the long hair is strange. It has also been suggested that he could represent the young Raphael. The portraits of Titian and

Michelangelo (died 1564) were taken from existing portraits, and that of Giulio Clovio follows closely El Greco's portrait of his friend in the Naples Museum (Plate iv), painted *c.* 1571. El Greco does continue to include portraits in his paintings of religious subjects, but here there is no proper connection with the subject matter. El Greco first painted the subject in Venice, some years earlier, in the small signed panel in Washington, and he was to take it up again, much later, in Spain, and adhere closely to his original design (Plate xxxi). As with the *Christ healing the Blind*, inspiration for the composition as a whole is from Tintoretto. The main central group, however, is very close to a Michelangelo design, known in drawings, and also in Venusti's painting after Michelangelo's design (National Gallery, London). The figure of the woman walking with a child could be a reminiscence of a similar motif in Raphael's tapestry cartoon, the *Distributing of Alms at the Golden Gate*. The two men in conversation, who also appear in the middle distance of *Christ healing the Blind*, have become a grand subsidiary motif, and again hint at acquaintance with Raphael. The larger forms of the architecture also derive from Raphael and Rome, and are consonant with the grander conception of the one integrated action of the main group of figures. This is the most splendid painting produced before his removal to Italy.

Plate vi *The Pietà* (The Lamentation of Christ). Tempera on panel. 11½ × 8 in. (29 × 20 cm.). Signed. 1571 – 76. Museum of Art, Philadelphia, Pennsylvania.

A translation in paint of Michelangelo's late sculptured group of the *Pietà* in Florence Cathedral, at the time in Rome. The pattern and the feeling are the same. The figures of the Dead Christ, His Mother, Saint Mary Magdalene and Joseph of Arimathea make one compact group. Michelangelo achieved this by his new treatment of form; El Greco by paint, by employing broader, more continuous passages of colour. The more vivid colours of Rome combine with the richer palette of Venice to convey the intensity of expression demanded by the subject. The horizontal composition of Venice, more suited to a narrative type of subject than to the single image, is given up and is only very rarely found appropriate in Spain. In the collection of the Hispanic Society of America is a larger version of the subject, unsigned, in oil on canvas, for which this may be a study. The subject is not repeated in Spain.

Plates vii, viii and **ix** Paintings for the High Altar and side altars of the Church of Santo Domingo el Antiguo,

Toledo, begun in the spring of 1577 and completed in the summer of 1579.

Plate vii   *The Assumption of the Virgin.*   Oil on canvas. 158 × 90 in. (401 × 229 cm.). Signed and dated 1577. Art Institute, Chicago.

Painted for the central panel of the High Altarpiece of the church of Santo Domingo el Antiguo, Toledo, the commission which brought him to Spain. This, the first work executed in Spain, is the only painting by El Greco bearing the date of its execution. It is the first large-scale painting by his hand. There is a clear reminiscence of Venetian paintings of the subject, and specifically of Titian's early masterpiece in the church of the Frari in Venice, but the treatment is his own. The Virgin rises as from a chalice formed by the two unified groups on either side of the open tomb, which introduce and extend motifs developed in his *Cleansing of the Temple* and *Healing of the Blind.* A complete unity is achieved in this bi-partite composition, in which the circle of Apostles, with its contained and concentrated internal movement, or emotion, is continued in the circle of angels with their easy and sympathetic movement around the rising figure of the Virgin. There is a sustained rhythm of the expressions, gestures and surface treatment within each group, and an easy and inevitable connection of one group with another. This is achieved essentially by paint, the measured relationship of the passages of colour over the surface. This also explains his treatment of the draperies, which has its own logic, has no suggestion of conflict, but is also not concerned with disclosing the anatomy beneath. No other version of the subject is known, but the painting may be regarded as the forerunner of the related composition of the *Immaculate Conception,* a subject more compatible with El Greco's mystical approach to the Universe.

Plate viii   *The Trinity.*   Oil on canvas. 118 × 70½ in. (300 × 179 cm.). Not signed. 1577—79. Museo del Prado, Madrid.

Painted for the attic of the High Altarpiece of Santo Domingo el Antiguo, Toledo, to go above the Assumption (Plate vii). Probably painted 1577—78, following the *Assumption.* Here the reference is to Rome, rather than to Venice, and specifically to Michelangelo, developing the motif of the *Pietà* (Plate vi). The general scheme of the composition of the *Trinity,* however, refers to Dürer's engraving of the same subject. The composition continues that of the *Assumption* below, slowing down the upward movement which finally comes to rest in the supported shoulders of Christ. Form is more in evidence here than in the *Assumption,* especially in the Michelangelesque motif of the naked Christ, and it is only later that he treats his figures with the same freedom as draperies. Here the suggestion of weight in the supported Dead Christ is appropriate. El Greco was not to repeat this subject.

Plate ix   *The Resurrection.* Oil on canvas. 82½ × 50½ in. (210 × 128 cm.). Not signed. 1577—79. Church of Santo Domingo el Antiguo, Toledo.

Painted for the side altar on the Epistle side (right) of the church, and still in place. Probably painted 1578—79, following the completion of the High Altarpiece. The presence of Saint Ildefonso, the patron Saint of Toledo, was stipulated in the documents. Diego de Castilla, the Dean of Toledo Cathedral, is probably represented in this figure, which certainly is a portrait. The figure assists in setting an ideal plane for the enacting of the mystic event. El Greco has eliminated the intrusion of an incongruous space. The ground running parallel with the plane of the action produces no conflict. The rhythm of the passages of colour and light over the surface helps to hold together the composition, with its dramatic split revealing the figure of the Risen Christ. What suggestions remain of an ordinary conception of space, of corporeality and of a schematic quality of composition, disappear in his final version of the subject (Plate xxiv).

Plate x   *The 'Espolio'*   (Disrobing of Christ). Oil on canvas. 112 × 68 in. (285 × 173 cm.). Signed. 1577—79. Sacristy, Toledo Cathedral.

Commenced in the summer of 1577, and completed in the spring of 1579, for the High Altar of the Sacristy of the Cathedral, where it still hangs. A document of 2nd July 1577 referring to this painting is the earliest record of El Greco in Spain. El Greco has produced one of the most dignified and moving portrayals of Christ in art. The powerful effect of the painting especially depends upon his original and forceful use of colour. Something of the effect of the grand images of the Saviour in Byzantine art is recalled. The motif of the crowding round Christ suggests an acquaintance with the works of the Northern artist, Bosch; the figure preparing the Cross could be derived from the similar figure bending forward in Raphael's tapestry cartoon of the *Miraculous Draught of Fishes.* This is, however, the last time that there are any hints of specific borrowings. A small, signed version of the *Espolio,* at Upton Park, Warwickshire, the original preliminary model is probably for the large painting. Many other versions exist, but few can be by El Greco. The only occasion that he treated the subject was for the Cathedral, but the type of Christ created in the *Espolio* is taken up in the related subject of *Christ carrying the Cross* (Plate xxxiii), and in other representations of Christ. The initial reception of the painting, when seen by the artists brought to value it, was that it was beyond appraisal. After the artist's death, the first real recognition of the painting was some two centuries later when Goya painted his *Taking of Christ* for the same sacristy.

Plate xi *Lady with a fur* (Jerónima de las Cuevas?). Oil on canvas. 24½ × 20 in. (62 × 51 cm.). Not signed. 1577—80. Mrs Maxwell MacDonald, Pollok House, Glasgow.

Most likely a portrait of Jerónima de las Cuevas, his life-long companion in Spain, and the mother of his son, Jorge Manuel. The style belongs to his first years in Spain. The treatment, with the greater continuity of brushstroke, is related to that of his portrait of *Vincentio Anastagi* of his last years in Italy, and to his first paintings in Spain. The fact that he painted very few female portraits, the intimate quality of the portrait, the apparent age of the sitter, and the correspondence in time with the setting up of the household, all point to the identification as Doña Jerónima. Cézanne's copy of the painting (1879—80; Pellerin collection, Paris) heralded the ultimate recognition of the artist.

Plate xii *The Adoration of the Name of Jesus* ('Dream of Philip II'). Oil on canvas. 74½ × 55 in. (190 × 140 cm.). Signed. 1578—79. Chapter House, Monastery of the Escorial.

The earliest reference to the painting appears in Francisco de los Santos, *Descripción . . . del Escorial*, published in 1657, when it was in the sacristy of the Pantheon: ' . . . commonly called the "Glory of El Greco" on account of the Glory above, but there is also represented, below, Purgatory and Hell, and on the other side, the Church Militant, with an immense number of the Faithful in adoration, raising their hands and eyes to Heaven, and among them Philip II; in the middle of the Glory is the Name of Jesus adored by Angels . . . signifying the words of Saint Paul *In Nomine Jesu omne genu flectatur Caelestium, Terrestrium, & Infernorum*' (Saint Paul, Epistle to the Philippians, II, 10). The subject, then, is the Adoration of the Name of Jesus, a Jesuit counterpart of the Adoration of the Lamb, and incorporates the 'Church Militant', represented by the Holy League. The

popular title, the 'Dream of Philip II', is more recent. The painting must certainly have been made for Philip II, but no documents refer to it and it is strangely not mentioned by Sigüenza in his description of the Escorial, published in 1608. The occasion of the commission may well have been the death of Juan of Austria in 1577, and the translation of his body to the Pantheon in 1578. The painting was in the Pantheon when los Santos described it. Juan of Austria was the general in charge of the forces of the Holy League at the victory of Lepanto in 1571. The three members of the Holy League, Spain, Venice and the Papal States are represented by the three kneeling figures of Philip II, Doge Mocenigo and Pope Pius V, and the one prominent figure of the foreground group, kneeling in heroic pose, and holding a sword, can represent no other than the general in charge at Lepanto. It is an ideal representation, while the King, Pope and Doge are actual portraits. Sir Anthony Blunt first suggested that this *Adoration of the Name of Jesus* was an allegory of the Holy League (the 'Church Militant'), and was possibly commissioned for the tomb of the Spanish General in the Pantheon. That is, it was more in the nature of a private commission for the King, and not part of the scheme of decoration of the Escorial. This could explain the absence of documents. The spirit of universal adoration is brilliantly conveyed. For the general arrangement of the painting, El Greco seems, appropriately, to have referred to his *Allegory of a Christian Knight*, of the Modena Triptych (Plate i). The figures of the King, Pope, Doge and Juan of Austria take the place of the three Theological Virtues. The Jaws of Hell and the representation of Purgatory are very similar. The figure of Don Juan of Austria is inspired by Michelangelo. So special a commission could hardly have been the subject of a test-piece for the Escorial as has generally been suggested. *The Martyrdom of Saint Maurice and His Legions* was a specific commission (and the only commission) for the Escorial. The study for the painting, a small signed panel, is in the National Gallery, London.

Plate xiii *The Martyrdom of Saint Maurice and his Legions*. Oil on canvas. 176½ × 118½ in. (448 × 301 cm.). Signed. 1579/80—82. Chapter House, Monastery of El Escorial.

The signature appears on the paper held in the mouth of a serpent (the spirit of evil, or of the Earth). The large painting was commissioned by Philip II, late 1579 or early 1580, for the chapel of the Saint in the church of the Escorial. The earliest reference is the King's order to the Prior, dated 25th April 1580 to provide the artist with materials, 'especially ultramarine', to enable him to carry out the commission given some time ago. El Greco had clearly already decided upon the dominant colour for the painting. The painting was completed by 16th November 1582, when it was delivered to the Escorial. The commission was probably prompted by the death of Navarrete in 1579, who left unfulfilled the greater part of his commission to provide paintings for the thirty-six altars of the church. The painting did not satisfy the King, Cincinato was commissioned to paint a substitute for the chapel and El Greco received no further commissions from the King. The subject of the martyrdom of the soldier Saint with his legions, for his refusal to worship the pagan gods. was appropriate for the Escorial, the real centre of the crusade for the Faith. This subject expresses the conviction of faith that inspired the crusade; the *Allegory of the Holy League* (Plate xii), the militant spirit of the crusade itself. The ecstatic character of this 'invitation to death' (Ortega y Gasset) is expressed. The physical side of the martyrdom is not emphasised, is no more than symbolised by the small group on the left comprising the one martyred figure, the figure, in the pose of his Christ of the Baptism, awaiting martyrdom and the grand figure in back-view of the executioner. The impression of the ranks of the Saint's army awaiting martyrdom is similar to that of the multitude in adoration in the *Adoration of the Name of Jesus*. The two paintings are related in composition, and in their expression of devotional fervour. The grand group of Saint Maurice and his companions owes much to the heroic figure style of Rome. There is however no emphasis on weight or volume. There is also no emphasis on spatial depth.

Plate xiv   *Saint Sebastian.* Oil on canvas. 75½ × 58¼ in. (192 × 148 cm.). Signed. *c.* 1580. Sacristy, Palencia Cathedral.

The Saint abandoned after his martyrdom and presumed death. The style is that of around 1580. The frontal placing of the nude figure and treatment of the forms avoids a three-dimensional emphasis. The greater prominence of the setting — and of actual depth, in the vista on the right — compared with the paintings for Santo Domingo, the Cathedral and the Escorial, depends on the subject. In comparable representations of Saints, as of the Magdalene or Saint Jerome in the wilderness, he continues to indicate a setting. Where the image alone is demanded, as in his series of Apostles, a setting is omitted. In this painting the forms of tree and rock and the silhouette of the foliage are made to continue the plane of the figure. It is perhaps the natural sequence

in the process of dematerialisation that the more flexible elements, the draperies, preceded the nude figure and natural forms. El Greco did not use the pose again for a Saint Sebastian. A related figure is the Christ in the Prado *Baptism* (Plate xxii) of some fifteen to twenty years later; the *Saint Jerome* (Plate xlvi) of his last year shows the culmination of this development. The compositional motif of the pose, with the outstretched leg taking the movement upwards appears in the *Adoration of the Shepherds* of similar date, and indeed in El Greco's work is first met in the *Adoration* of the Modena Triptych (Plate i).

Plate xv   *Saint Mary Magdalene.* Oil on canvas. 42½ × 34¼ in. (108 × 87 cm.). Not signed. 1580 — 85. Rockhill Nelson Gallery of Art, Kansas City.

The Penitent Magdalene is one of the most recurrent themes. She and Saint Veronica, both close to Christ and His Passion, are the only female Saints he treated. A comparison with the *Saint Sebastian* indicates a somewhat later dating. An earlier version, signed, of identical pose, is in the Art Museum, Worcester, U.S.A.; and one of the final representations is the ecstatic Magdalene in the Valdés Collection, Bilbao. The painting is based on a Titian type, although there is no record that he portrayed the Saint before he moved to Spain.

Plate xvi   *The Virgin of the Immaculate Conception and Saint John.* Oil on canvas. 93 × 46½ in. (237 × 118 cm.). Not signed. *c.* 1585. Museo de Santa Cruz, Toledo.

The Virgin of the Immaculate Conception is related to Saint John's Vision of the Apocalypse: *And there appeared a great wonder in Heaven: a woman clothed with the sun, and the moon under her feet, and upon her head a crown of twelve stars: and she being with child cried, . . . And she brought forth a man child, who was to rule all nations with a rod of iron: and her child was caught up unto God, and to his throne . . .* (Revelation, xii). The roses, iris, olive, palm, portal and throne all belong to the iconography of the Immaculate Conception. The twelve stars have been omitted. This subject, related in composition to that of the Assumption of the Virgin, with which it is sometimes confused, was more suited to El Greco's genius, more in sympathy with the expression of the purely supernatural image. In Spain, he avoids anything that can be related to mundane actions or events, which would detract from the expression of the supernatural. The rather angular and schematic quality of the design is appropriate to the image, and captures something of the grand effect of Byzantine designs. The mandorla shape, belonging to this image — the clothing with the sun — is again introduced effectively in the *Burial of the Count of Orgaz* (Plate xvii). The general pattern is retained in the splendid late painting in the Thyssen-Bornemisza Collection, Lugano. The subject inspired the great masterpiece of his last years (Plate xliii).

Plate xvii *The Burial of the Count of Orgaz.* Oil on canvas. 179 × 141 in. (480 × 360 cm.). Signed. 1586. Church of Santo Tomé, Toledo.

The contract for the painting is dated 18th March 1586. El Greco agreed to finish the painting by Christmas of the same year. This commission again resulted in litigation over the valuation, the final outcome of which was that the artist accepted the amount of the original valuation, 1200 *ducados*. The painting illustrates a popular local legend. In 1312, a certain Don Gonzalo Ruíz, native of Toledo, and Señor of the town of Orgaz, died (the family received the title of Count, by which he is generally known, only later). He was a pious man who, among other charitable acts, left moneys for the enlargement and adornment of the church of Santo Tomé (El Greco's parish church). At his burial, Saint Stephen and Saint Augustine intervened to lay him to rest. The occasion for the commission of the painting for the chapel in which the Señor was buried, was the resumption of the tribute payable to the church by the town of Orgaz, which had been withheld for over two centuries. The painting remains in the chapel — the actual scene of the event — for which it was ordered. Already in 1588, people flocked to see the painting. This immediate popular reception depended, however, on the 'life-like portrayal of the notable men of Toledo of the time'. Indeed, this painting is sufficient to rank El Greco among the few great portrait painters. Nowadays the painting can communicate to us a whole society and age, as perhaps no other single work of art can, and at the same time offer us one of the great marvels of painting. It was the custom for the eminent and noble men of the town to assist at the burial of the high-born, and it was stipulated in the contract that the scene should be represented in this way. Without the contemporary confirmation, it would be clear that all are portraits. Unfortunately, there is no record of the identity of the sitters. Andrés Núñez, the parish priest, and a friend of El Greco's, who was responsible for the commission, is certainly the figure on the extreme right. The artist himself can be recognised in the *caballero* third from the left, immediately above the head of Saint Stephen. The artist's son acts as the young page. The signature of the artist appears on the handkerchief in the pocket of the young boy, and by a strange conceit it is followed by the date '1578' — the year of Jorge Manuel's birth, and certainly not the date of the painting. The boy points to the body of the deceased, thus bringing together birth and death. The painting is very clearly divided into two zones, the heavenly above and the terrestrial below, but there is little feeling of duality. The upper and lower zones are brought together compositionally (e.g., by the standing figures, by their varied participation in the earthly and heavenly event, by the torches, cross, . . .). The grand circular mandorla-like pattern of the two Saints descended from Heaven echoes the pattern formed by the Virgin and Saint John the Baptist, and the action is given explicit expression. The point of equilibrium is the outstretched hand poised in the void between the two Saints, whence the mortal body descends, and the Soul, in the medieval form of a transparent and naked child, is taken up by the angel to be received in Heaven. The supernatural appearance of the Saints is enhanced by the splendour of colour and light of their gold vestments. The powerful cumulative emotion expressed by the group of participants is suffused and sustained through the composition by the splendour, variety and vitality of the colour and effects of light. This is the first completely personal work by the artist. There are no longer any references to Roman or Venetian formulas or motifs. He has succeeded in eliminating any description of space. There is no ground, no horizon, no sky and no perspective. Accordingly, there is no conflict, and a convincing expression of a supernatural space is achieved. This is the beginning of his real development, and the process of dematerialisation and spiritualisation continues.

Plate xviii *The Coronation of the Virgin.* Oil on canvas. 41½ × 31½ in. (105 × 80 cm.). Signed. 1591. Museo de Santo Cruz, Toledo.

Painted for the High Altar of the parish church of Talavera la Vieja (Toledo Province). The contract for the decoration of the chapel is dated 1591. In this painting El Greco has set the general pattern for the subject, to be repeated in the Chapel of San José, Toledo (1597−99), and at Illescas (1603−05; see Plate xxxix).

Plate xix *Saint Francis and Saint Andrew.* Oil on canvas. 65 × 44 in. (167 × 113 cm.). Signed. *c.* 1595. Museo del Prado, Madrid.

El Greco would have been aware of the grand series of pairs of Saints painted by Navarrete for the chapels of the Church of the Escorial, the commission interrupted by the latter's death in 1579. From the time of the *Burial of the Count of Orgaz*, El Greco began to create his own images of the different Saints. Once a pattern was created, he kept closely to it. The pairing of Saints — the juxtaposition of two separate personalities, with their different spiritual significance — accentuates the individual characters. Saint Peter and Saint Paul, the two Saint Johns, ...ore obvious juxtapositions, but he also brought ...ner such unlikely characters as in the present painting — the one, the somewhat austere Apostle and Martyr of the time of Christ; the other, the ecstatic and 'gentle' Saint of the Middle Ages. The landscape also is double. ...he Saint Francis derives from the figure on the left of the *Burial of the Count of Orgaz* (Plate xvii), and has become more spiritualised; the Saint Andrew is the same type as that of the Talavera painting of 1591, and the gesture is a remarkable development of the similar gesture of the Saint Maurice, in the Escorial painting (Plate xiv), and eventually, indeed, can be traced back to the early *Healing of the Blind* (Plate ii).

Plate xx The Annunciation. Tempera on panel 10⅜ × 7⅝ in. (26.5 × 19.5 cm.). Unsigned. 1569 − 1570. Museo del Prado, Madrid.

This very small panel is probably the most completely Venetian of his paintings, and, almost certainly, was finished shortly before leaving for Rome at the end of 1570. With its comparitively robust figures and the perspective of its pavement sharply receding into the background, it provides a good contrast with his later Spanish works. *The Annunciation* was one of the themes most in harmony with his genius, inspiring some of his most splendid paintings. A much larger version, often thought of as his finest interpretation of this subject was carried out as part of the series for the Colegio de Doña María, Madrid, and appears to have been the central painting of the retable of the high altar.

Plates xxi, xxii, xxiii, xxiv and xxv
Paintings for the high altar of the Colegio de Doña María, Madrid. Begun December 1596, completed July 1600. The retable no longer exists, and the paintings are dispersed. The subjects of the paintings of the retable are not recorded, but according to Ceán (*Diccionario de Bellas Artes*, 1800) they illustrated the Life of Christ. For reasons of size, style, and subject matter, the following paintings probably came from the retable: the *Annunciation*, the widest painting, in the centre (the church was dedicated to the Virgin of the Annunciation); the *Adora-*

tion of the Shepherds and the *Baptism of Christ*, two paintings of the same size, on the left and right of the *Annunciation*; the *Crucifixion* above the *Annunciation*; and the *Resurrection* and *Pentecost*, another pair of identical size, flanking the *Crucifixion* (the whole forming a retable of a type known in the Escorial). Such an arrangement gives a chronological sequence to the events of the Life of Christ. The payment of 6000 *ducados* (for the paintings and retable) indicate a large commission. Small versions, probably models, exist for the three paintings more generally accepted as belonging to the retable, the *Annunciation*, the *Adoration of the Shepherds* and the *Baptism of Christ*.

Plate xxi The Adoration of the Shepherds. Oil on canvas. 136 × 54 in. (346 × 137 cm.). Signed. 1596 − 1600. Rumanian National Museum, Bucharest.

Probably originally on the left of the retable of the Colegio de Doña María, and painted following the *Annunciation*. A small version, possibly the model for the large painting, is in the Galleria Corsini, Rome. The scrolls borne by the angels bear the inscription in Latin: *Glory to God in the highest, and on earth peace, goodwill towards men* (Luke II, 14); another popular subject in El Greco's repertoire, painted throughout his life. It was one of the subjects of the *Modena Triptych* (Plate i), and of his first commission in Spain, that for the church of Santo Domingo el Antiguo, and was the subject chosen for his own burial chapel in Santo Domingo (Fig. 6). A comparison with the earlier painting of the same subject in Santo Domingo shows the advance made in the proces sof developing a style appropriate to the expression of the supernatural. There is no reference to the ordinary conception of space of this world, there are no allusions to the corporal quality of the figures, whose gestures also belong to the realm of imagination and not to that of ordinary experience. Light is the important dematerialising and expressive element in this painting. The Santo Domingo painting can still be related to a human event.

Plate xxii The Baptism of Christ. Oil on canvas. 137 × 56 in. (350 × 144 cm.). Signed. 1596 − 1600. Museo del Prado, Madrid.

Probably originally on the right of the retable of the Colegio de Doña María, balancing the *Adoration of the Shepherds* (Plate xxi), and painted at the same time. A small version, possibly the model for the large painting, is in the Galleria Corsini, Rome. A later development of this subject, only treated once before, in the *Modena Triptych* (Plate i), is the painting for the Hospital de San

Juan Bautista, Toledo, probably completed after his death by Jorge Manuel. The pose of the Christ is related to that of the *Saint Sebastian* of *c.* 1580 (Plate xiv). The bipartite composition can be related to the *Burial of the Count of Orgaz* (Plate xvii), the portraits giving place to the range of angels. The splendid ecstatic figure of the angel, between the Baptist and Christ, is one of a number of such symbols that he began to introduce into his painting. If his figures — the actual participants in the action — become increasingly dematerialised, these new symbols appear as emotions materialised in gesture and colour.

Plate xxiii *The Crucifixion*. Oil on canvas. 123 × 66½ in. (312 × 169 cm.). Signed. 1596 – 1600. Museo del Prado, Madrid.

Christ on the Cross, at the moment of expiration, with the Virgin and Saint John, and at the foot of the Cross, the Magdalene. Probably originally above the *Annunciation*, in the retable of the Colegio of Doña María. This painting and the Annunciation are the two widest of the series. Already, in Santo Domingo el Antiguo, the artist had sensibly related together in composition the two central paintings of the high altar, the *Assumption* and *Trinity* (Plates vii and viii). Again, there is this compositional relationship of the two paintings, but there is also something more in this bringing together of the two so diverse yet intimately related themes of the Virgin's reception of the Holy Ghost, and Christ's giving up of the Holy Ghost. One subject represents one of the Joys of the Virgin, and the other incorporates one of Her Griefs. Each painting is divided horizontally in three. The figure of Christ of the Expiration is a continuation upwards of the central zone of the *Annunciation* with the Flames and the Dove; the figure of the Archangel Gabriel has its counterpart in the figure of Saint John; and the Virgin of Joy appears above as the Virgin of Grief. This painting of the *Crucifixion* is one of the great interpretations of the subject in painting and almost inevitably brings to mind two other great Crucifixions, Grünewald's of the Isenheim Altar and Giotto's of the Arena Chapel. El Greco has introduced more of those symbols embodying spiritual emotions: the clamouring angels with outstretched arms encircling the Body of Christ — strangely recalling Giotto's painting — and the remarkable figure of the angel at the foot of the Cross.

Plate xxiv *The Resurrection*. Oil on canvas. Originally arched top. 108½ × 50 in. (275 × 127 cm.). Signed. 1596 to 1600. Museo del Prado, Madrid.

Probably painted for the Colegio de Doña María, Madrid. It is of the same size and shape as the *Pentecost* (Plate xxv), to which it was almost certainly a pair. The place of these two paintings in the chapel is more difficult to decide. The *Resurrection* was almost certainly on the left and the *Pentecost* on the right, because of their relationship in meaning with the *Nativity* (Plate xxi) and the *Baptism* (Plate xxii), respectively. If they were placed above these two paintings, the narrower format would correspond with the upper range of paintings. This and the *Pentecost* would have been the last of the paintings executed for the Colegio. Only one other painting of the subject by El Greco is known, that for Santo Domingo el Antiguo (Plate ix). This painting and the *Adoration of the Shepherds* are higher in proportion to their width than the corresponding paintings in Santo Domingo el Antiguo. Again El Greco has created one of the greatest interpretations of the subject in art. It can, perhaps, only be compared with the great masterpiece by Piero della Francesca. Light is the important element in this image of the Risen Christ, as it was in the *Adoration of the Shepherds*, but of a different quality. The movement has an incomparably greater force than in the Santo Domingo painting and has nothing of the sharp explosive quality of the earlier work. The movement is not dissipated, but is contained and concentrated. The figures now are vehicles of movement and light. It is interesting to compare the treatment of the classical 'draperies' of the soldier at the base of the composition with those of the saintly warriors of the *Martyrdom of Saint Maurice and his Legions* (Plate xiv).

Plate xxv *The Pentecost*. Oil on canvas. Originally arched top. 108½ × 50 in. (275 × 127 cm.). Signed. 1596 – 1600? Museo del Prado, Madrid.

Certainly a pair to the *Resurrection* (Plate xxiv) and almost certainly painted for the Colegio de Doña María. The two paintings appear to be of the same date, that is, the last to be painted for the Colegio. There are, however, certain passages in this painting that suggest overpainting or finishing by another hand (Jorge Manuel's?), which could point to a separate contract for this pair of paintings for the college. He was late in finishing the commission and there were difficulties in collecting moneys from the College — was the last of the series left unfinished, and completed later by his son? The Apostle second from the right is certainly a portrait of the artist, and the same portrait appears in the *Marriage of the Virgin* (Plate xlvii), one of his last works.

Plates xxvi, xxvii and xxviii
Paintings for the high altar and side altars of the Chapel of San José, Toledo. Begun end 1597; completed end 1599. The Chapel dedicated to Saint Joseph, Saint Teresa's favourite Saint — '*the Father of my Soul*' — for it was the original intention of the founder, Martín Ramírez (d. 1595) to build a chapel for her (d. 1582). The paintings for the high altar (still in place) were the *Saint Joseph and the Christ Child* (Plate xxvi), and above, the *Coronation of the Virgin*; and, for the side chapels, the *Saint Martin and the Beggar* and the *Virgin and Child with Saints* (Plates xxvii and xxviii).

Plate xxvi *Saint Joseph and the Christ Child*. Oil on canvas. 114 × 58 in. (289 × 147 cm.). Signed. 1597 − 99. Chapel of San José, Toledo.

The central painting of the high altar and probably the first of the series to be painted for the Chapel of San José. Saint Joseph is shown as a figure of trust and protection to the Christ Child, who indicates the way. The colours, the rhythm of the tower-like figure of Joseph, express perfectly the meaning of the painting. There is no 'mannerist' ambiguity in the relationship of figure to setting. The subject is a parallel to that of Saint Anne teaching the Virgin, and is an extract from the theme of the Christ Child walking between the Virgin and Saint Joseph. It is at this time that El Greco begins to include a view of Toledo in his paintings. The view here is that of the Metropolitan Museum painting (Plate xxix; none of the view is lost, for the figures merely divide it in two). The small signed version in the Museo de Santa Cruz s probably the model for the painting.

Plate xxvii *Saint Martin and the Beggar*. Oil on canvas. 75¼ × 38½ in. (191 × 98 cm.). Signed. 1597 − 99. National Gallery, Washington, D.C.

Saint Martin shares his cloak with the beggar. Painted for the side altar, on the Gospel side (left) of the Chapel of San José, and probably after the paintings for the main altar. The bridge over the Tagus, as it appears in the *Saint Joseph and the Christ Child* (Plate xxvi), is discernible near the raised hoof of the horse. The dedication to Saint Martin is probably a reference to the founder, Martín Ramírez.

Plate xxviii *The Virgin and Child, with Saint Martina and Saint Agnes*. Oil on canvas. 76 × 41½ in. (193 × 105 cm.). Signed (with initials on the head of the lion). 1597 − 99. National Gallery, Washington, D.C.

Saint Martina with the lion; Saint Agnes with the Lamb. Painted for the side altar, on the Epistle side (right) of the Chapel of San José, and probably after the paintings for the main altar. The more schematic composition is appropriate to the image, but the angularity of the early *Immaculate Conception* (Plate xvi) has gone. The image of the Virgin and Child, alone or as a Holy Family, was one of El Greco's most popular subjects, and a number of versions follow this basic pattern for the Virgin and her Child. The inclusion of Saint Martina is possibly again a reference to the name of the founder.

Plate xxix *Toledo*. Oil on canvas. 47½ × 41¾ in. (121 × 106 cm.). Signed. 1597 − 99. Metropolitan Museum, New York.

The fact that an identical view appears in the *Saint Joseph and the Christ Child* (Plate xxvi) suggests that the painting was conceived in connection with the San José commission (1597 − 99). From that time, the town features in many of his paintings: in the *Laocöon* (Plate xxx), the *Christ in Agony on the Cross* (Plate xxxv), the *Immaculate Conception* (Plate xliii; again repeating this view), in all of which it takes on an apocalyptical character appropriate to the themes. In his late *Saint John the Baptist in the Wilderness* (M.H. de Young Memorial Museum, San Francisco) the landscape of the Escorial is appropriately introduced. This is one of the earliest independent landscapes in Western art and one of the most dramatic and individual landscapes ever painted. It is not just a 'View of Toledo', although the topographical details are correct; neither is it 'Toledo at night' or 'Toledo in a storm', other titles which have been attached to the painting: it is simply 'Toledo', but Toledo given a universal meaning — a spiritual portrait of the town. In introducing the view into his paintings he acknowledges how much his art owed to the inspiration of the town, until a few years before the great Imperial Capital and still the great ecclesiastical and cultural centre of Spain — the town isolated on the plain of Castile which he had made his new home, so far from the island of his birth. El Greco painted another view of the town as an independent subject, the *View and Plan of Toledo* in the Museo del Greco, Toledo, with the vision of Saint Ildefonso and the Virgin poised above the cathedral (Fig. 5).

Plate xxx *The Laocöon*. Oil on canvas. 56 × 76 in. (142 × 193 cm.). Not signed. 1600 − 10. National Gallery, Washington, D.C.

In the background, a view of Toledo, as Troy, and the Trojan Horse. El Greco would have known the sculptured group in Rome, uncovered at the beginning of the sixteenth century, but more significantly he would have known the original story, which he has interpreted in an entirely independent way. This is the only known painting of classical subject matter by El Greco, and he does seem to give it a special spiritual meaning. The horizontal format is uncharacteristic of his works in Spain, which become increasingly more elevated in composition and spirit. The essential verticality of the composition is made clear, however, by the high horizon and the upward movement of the flanking figures. The view of Toledo appears to have been taken from the same viewpoint as that of the Metropolitan Museum painting (Plate xxix), which it continues to the right, the two together completing the panorama of the town. The panoramic *View and plan of Toledo* in the Museo del Greco, Toledo, is taken from a different viewpoint. Recent cleaning has uncovered a third figure in the group on the right, which El Greco had overpainted.

Plate xxxi *Christ driving the Traders from the Temple* (The Cleansing of the Temple). Oil on canvas. 41¾ × 51 in. (106 × 130 cm.). Not signed. *c.* 1600. National Gallery, London.

A late version of the subject treated twice in his Italian years. The scene is restricted to the main group, which follows almost exactly that of the original design of some forty years back (Plate v), which in its turn used a Michelangelo design. A greater expressive force is attained by this concentration in the one group, and is infinitely enhanced by the vitality of the colour and handling. The disturbing effect of the empty space on the right of his earlier versions, and of the recessional perspective of the tiled pavement and the vista through the arch has been eliminated. The three-dimensional character of the figures and space is not described: the event alone is expressed, and creates its own space. The episodal type of subject is unusual for El Greco in Spain — he does not repeat the *Christ healing the Blind* (Plate iii), the possible sequel to this event. The subject was, of course, of special relevance to the age of the Counter-Reformation. In any event, El Greco has raised it above the merely dogmatic or episodal. The Venetian motif of the reclining female figure of the early versions has been substituted by the male figure bending down, which may again be a recollection from Raphael's tapestry cartoon of the *Miraculous Draught of Fishes*. The reliefs to the left and right of the arch represent the Expulsion from Paradise, an Old Testament parallel of the Expulsion from the Temple, and the Sacrifice of Isaac, less easily connected with the subject. In this late version, El Greco has introduced the

overthrown 'tables of the moneylenders and the seats of those who sold doves' (St Matthew XXI, 12). A number of late versions exist, of which the National Gallery painting is the finest example. The splendid small version in the Frick Collection, New York, is probably the study for the larger painting.

Plate xxxii *Cardinal Fernando Niño de Guevara*. Oil on canvas. 76½ × 51¼ in. (194 × 130 cm.). Signed. *c.* 1600 Metropolitan Museum, New York.

Niño de Guevara (1541 – 1609), Cardinal 1596, Inquisitor-General 1600, Archbishop of Seville 1601. Probably painted *c.* 1600, when Inquisitor-General, and certainly before he became Archbishop of Seville. One of a number of eminent ecclesiastics of Toledo portrayed by El Greco, and one of his finest portraits. The splendour and richness of colour is appropriate to the character and rank of the sitter. The frontal turn of the pose concentrates attention on the figure.

Plate xxxiii *Christ carrying the Cross*. Oil on canvas. 42½ × 30¾ in. (108 × 78 cm.). Signed. 1600 – 05. Museo del Prado, Madrid.

El Greco treated the theme many times in Spain. The earliest date from soon after the *Espolio*, to which it is essentialy rellated. The subject of the *Espolio* is not repeated, but the Christ becomes the prototype for the Christ Carrying the Cross.

Plate xxxiv *The Annunciation*. Oil on canvas. 50½ × 32¾ in. (128 × 83 cm.). Not signed. 1600 – 10. Toledo Museum, Ohio.

The colour and ecstatic movement is of the utmost splendour and grace, appropriate to the presentation of this particular Mystery, one of El Greco's favourite themes. The painting is a later and simpler version of the subject painted for the Colegio de Doña María, Madrid.

Plate xxxv *Christ on the Cross*. Oil on canvas. 41 × 24½ in. (104 × 62 cm.). Signed. 1600 – 10. Art Museum, Cincinnati.

The Christ in Agony on the Cross, with a view of Toledo. Another — and finer — version, is in the Museum of Art, Cleveland, but with part of the landscape cut away. Christ on the Cross is left alone '*and there was a darkness over all the earth . . . and the sun was darkened, and the veil of the Temple was rent in the midst*' (St Luke, XXIII, 44 – 45), and he commends his spirit to His Lord. El Greco was in sympathy with the apocalyptical atmosphere of the theme. From the time of the San José paintings, El Greco often chose to include a view of Toledo in his paintings. It is in no way a naturalistic view, but is transformed as all else in his painting.

Plate xxxvi *Portrait of the artist's son, Jorge Manuel.* Oil on canvas. 32 × 21 in. (81 × 56 cm.). Signed. *c.* 1603. Museo Provincial, Seville.

Jorge Manuel appears about the same age as in the *Virgin of Charity* (Plate xxxviii), painted 1603 – 05, that is, when he was twenty-five to twenty-seven years old. The young gentleman, of a certain aristocratic mien, displays elegantly the tools of his craft. It is one of his most splendid portraits, but it is with difficulty that one relates the personality to that of the *Saint Luke.* Jorge Manuel was not a remarkable painter like his father.

Plate xxxvii *Saint Bernardino.* Oil on canvas. 106 × 56¾ in. (269 × 144 cm.). Signed. 1603. Museo del Greco, Toledo.

Painted for the high altar of the Colegio de San Bernardino, Toledo, between February and September, 1603. In the last decade or so of his life El Greco created a number of life-size, full-length standing Saints — *Saint John the Baptist* (De Young Memorial Museum, San Francisco); *Saint Peter* (El Escorial; Plate xlv); *Saint Ildefonso* (El Escorial) — which are among the most impressive of his works. A splendid motif is the group of three mitres, an attribute of the Saint.

Plates xxxviii, xxxix and xl Paintings for the High Altar of the church of the Hospital de la Caridad, Illescas (Toledo province), begun 1603 and completed 1605.

Plate xxxviii *The Virgin of Charity.* Oil on canvas. 61 × 48½ in. (155 × 123 cm.). Not signed. 1603 – 05. Hospital de la Caridad, Illescas.

Painted for the High Altar of the Church of the Hospital de la Caridad, and now placed in a side altar, balancing the *Saint Ildefonso* (Plate xli). El Greco was responsible for the whole of the decoration of the chapel, begun in 1603, and completed in 1605. All the portraits are of men of Toledo of his time. The ruffs had grown to rather exaggerated proportions in the twenty years from the time of the *Burial of the Count of Orgaz* (Plate xvii), and their introduction into the painting was censured by the Hospital authorities. At some time they were painted over, but have been recently restored. El Greco's son appears on the extreme right, at about the same age as in the portrait in Seville (Plate xxxvi).

Plate xxxix *The Coronation of the Virgin.* Oil on canvas. 64 × 86½ in. (163 × 220 cm.). Not signed. 1603 – 05. Hospital de la Caridad, Illescas.

Painted for the vault of the main chapel of the church, and now exhibited in the vestry. The pattern follows closely that of El Greco's first treatment of the subject at Talavera in 1591 (Plate xviii). The design is effectively adapted to the oval field and to a viewpoint from below, as are also the flanking circular paintings (Plate xl).

Plate xl *The Annunciation.* Oil on canvas. Diameter 50⅜ in. (128 cm.). Signed. 1603 – 05. Hospital de la Caridad, Illescas.

Painted for the lunette to the left of the *Coronation of the Virgin* (Plate xxxix), and now in the vestry of the church.

Plate xl *The Nativity.* Oil on canvas. Diameter 50⅜ in. (128 cm.). Signed. 1603 – 05. Hospital de la Caridad, Illescas.

Painted for the lunette to the right of the *Coronation of the Virgin* (Plate xxxix), and now in the vestry of the church.

Plate xli *Saint Ildefonso.* Oil on canvas. 62 × 40 in. (158 × 102 cm.). Signed. *c.* 1602 – 03 or *c.* 1607 – 09. Hospital de la Caridad, Illescas.

In the side altar on the left of the main chapel of the church, balancing the *Virgin of Charity* (Plate xxxviii). Its original place in the church is not known. The painting is not mentioned in the incomplete documentation for the decoration of the chapel, and if, as is probable, it was not painted at the same time, it cannot date much before June 1603, the date of the contract, and was more likely painted soon after the conclusion of litigation in August 1607. In its present position, it makes a grand pair to the *Virgin of Charity*, and is one of the most splendid of his 'portraits' of Saints. It is difficult, and perhaps not proper, to separate his portraits of Saints from his actual portraits. In both he employs all his means of spiritual or psychological expression. The legend is that Saint Ildefonso, the first Bishop of Toledo, presented an image of the Virgin of the Mantle to a foundation of his in Illescas. The Saint is portrayed before the same image, as he wrote his dissertation on the Purity of the Virgin. The state of inspiration is brilliantly expressed. There is an infinite distinction in expression between the hand poised with the pen in this 'portrait' and the similar motif in the portrait of his son (Plate xxxvi).

Plate xlii *Fray Hortensio Félix de Paravicino*. Oil on canvas. $44\frac{1}{2} \times 34$ in. (113×86 cm.). Signed. 1609—10. Museum of Fine Arts, Boston, Mass.

Portrait of his friend, the great Toledan poet (1580—1633). Paravicino, in his sonnet celebrating the portrait, tells us that it was painted when he was twenty-nine years of age. The complete frontality of the pose, the enormous simplicity, and the absence of any setting contribute to the feeling of spiritual presence, comparatively absent from the splendid portrait of Cardinal Guevara (Plate xxxii). The inspired rhythm and handling is no less a living thing than the man himself. It is one of the greatest masterpieces of portraiture and painting of all time.

Plate xliii *The Immaculate Conception*. Oil on canvas. $127\frac{1}{2} \times 65\frac{3}{4}$ in. (323×167 cm.). Not signed. 1607—13. Museo de Santa Cruz, Toledo.

The great masterpiece of his last manner. Painted for the High Altar of the Chapel of Oballe, San Vicente, Toledo, begun 1607, finished 1613. In the chapel until 1961, when it was transferred to the Museo de Santa Cruz. The painting certainly represents the Immaculate Conception, although it has often been referred to as an Assumption. The various attributes of the Virgin (roses, lilies, mirror, fountain of clear water) proper to the representantion of the Mystery, appear at the foot of the painting on the right. The same view of Toledo — but more ethereal — as in the painting in the Metropolitan Museum (Plate xxix), and in the *Saint Joseph and the Christ Child* (Plate xxvi) appears on the left. The painting is the grand culmination of El Greco's career. No artist has been able to express so convincingly the infinite: an infinity of colour and light, an infinity of movement and of space. This expression of the spiritual reality of the universe was only possible to attain by the uncompromising disengagement of his art from the material and transitory of this World. The earth, symbolised by Toledo, is already a phantom. From the burst of rose and white flowers at the base, a great upsurge of movement — of colour and light, in constant flux — commences, and increases in its rapture, and met by the light of the Dove, becomes all-pervading and infinite. One cannot halt the rhythm any more than in music, yet the grand central image is always present. It is perhaps the most remarkable realisation of spiritual ecstasy in painting, and one of the greatest masterpieces of colour. A single detail — the offering of flowers, the opening of a wing, the Virgin's mantle transfigured by light — is a moving experience in itself.

Plate xliv *The Visitation*. Oil on canvas. $38\frac{1}{4} \times 28$ in. (97×71 cm.). Not signed. 1610—14. Dumbarton Oaks, Washington, D.C..

Possibly a study for the circular painting in the vault of the Chapel of Oballe, San Vicente, Toledo, above the *Immaculate Conception* (Plate xliii) of the high altar, specified in the contract. It does seem that the painting was originally within a circle, and that the canvas has been cut at the left and right. It may well be the last work produced by the master, and the larger painting for the vault may never have been finished. The choice of subject of the Visitation is a reference to the name of the foundress of the Chapel, Isabel de Oballe. The process of dematerialisation is complete. There are only shapes, colour and light and the strange quality of the movement — of the 'meeting of two celestial bodies' (Camón Aznar, *Dominico Greco*, 1950).

Plate xlv *Saint Peter*. Oil on canvas. $81\frac{1}{2} \times 41\frac{1}{2}$ in. (207×105 cm.). Not signed. 1610—14. Monastery of El Escorial.

Probably, with the *Saint Ildefonso* also in the Escorial, painted for the Chapel of Oballe of the church of San Vicente, Toledo, to be placed to the left and right of the *Immaculate Conception* (Plate xliii), where for some time there have been old copies. The first Pope and the first Bishop of Toledo make a sensible pair. The infinite upward movement and powerful rhythm of this monolithic image express supremely the spiritual meaning of the 'Prince of the Apostles' the 'Rock upon which the Church was built'. This is the final expression of the Saint 'image'.

Plate xlvi *Saint Jerome Penitent*. Oil on canvas. $65\frac{1}{2} \times 43\frac{1}{2}$ in. (166×110 cm.). Not signed. 1610—14. National Gallery, Washington, D.C.

The final expression of his 'Saint in ecstasy' (compare Plates xiv, xv and xli). The pattern is still that of the *Saint Sebastian* (Plate xiv) of his first years in Spain, and it was employed also for the Christ of the *Baptism* (Plate xxii).

Plate xlvii *The Marriage of the Virgin*. $43\frac{1}{2} \times 32\frac{3}{4}$ in. (110×83 cm.). Not signed. 1610—14. Rumanian National Museum, Bucharest.

It is probable that the painting formed part of the decoration of the Hospital de la Caridad, dedicated to the Virgin. There is no mention of the painting in the original contract, but in any case, the nervous handling and almost complete dissolution of the forms belong to his very last years. The head third from the right is almost certainly a portrait of the aged painter, and is the same as that of the Apostle in a similar position in the *Pentecost* (Plate xxv), possibly completed at the same time.

Plate xlviii *Saint John's vision of the Apocalypse — The Opening of the Fifth Seal.* Oil on Canvas. 88¼ × 76½ in. (224 × 194 cm.). Not signed. 1610 – 14. Metropolitan Museum, New York.

One of his very last works. It is possibly connected with the commission, left unfinished on his death, for the Hospital de Tavera (Hospital de San Juan Bautista), Toledo. '*And when he had opened the fifth seal, I saw under the altar the souls of them that were slain for the word of God . . . And they cried with a loud voice . . . And white robes were given to every one of them . . .*' (Revelation of St John, VI, 9 – 11). The painting has been cut at the top, where there was possibly a representation of the Throne: '*And immediately I was in the spirit, and behold, a throne was set in heaven, and one sat on the throne . . . and round about the throne were four and twenty seats, and upon the seats I saw four and twenty elders . . . And I saw in the right hand of him that sat on the throne a book . . . sealed with seven seals . . .*' (Revelation of St John, IV – V). The transported figure of Saint John is on the left, his eyes turned towards the Glory above; his vision of the resurrected martyrs, on the right. The Spirit as 'a living flame, striving upwards', and this strange compatibility of infinite darkness and 'all-consuming light' is met with in the writings of the mystics of his time, Saint Teresa of Jesus and Saint John of the Cross. El Greco realises the apocalyptical vision in colour, light and movement. The painting fittingly closes his career.

11

III

IV

V

VI

VII

X

XIII

XIV

XVI

XVII

XVIII

XIX

XXI

XXII

XXIV

XXV

XXVI

XXVII

XXVIII

XXIX

XXX

XXXI

XXXII

XXXIII

XXXIV

XXXVII

XXXVIII

XXXIX

XLI

XLIII

XLIV

XLV

XLVI

XLVIII